D1304646

EDELMAN

and the Rise of Public Relations
by Franz Wisner

designed by Eight Communications

Copyright © 2012 by Daniel J. Edelman, Inc.

All rights reserved

Library of Congress Cataloging-in-Publication Data has been applied for
Wisner, Franz
Edeman and the Rise of Public Relations

Designed by Eight Communications

ISBN 978-0-9787522-0-0

CONTENTS

INTRODUCTION

The story of Dan Edelman, my father, is in many ways the story of modern public relations. It's an all-American tale about a son of immigrants, a child of the Depression, a young man who was part of the wave of men and women who served their country in World War II and then returned home to help create the most powerful economy the world has ever known.

My father's calling was a line of work that quenched his insatiable thirst for news and knowledge; it was a relatively new profession, with limitless potential for a bright, industrious communicator with a dream to start his own business: the burgeoning field of agency public relations.

Ever the entrepreneur and iconoclast, Dan Edelman built his firm and helped pioneer the public relations industry on his terms. While most agency founders chose New York, he put down his roots in Chicago. He created the television media tour while others focused on radio and print. He helped take modern public relations to China and the rest of Asia. While nearly every major P.R. firm sold out to advertising conglomerates, Dan remained true to his belief that public relations should be practiced independently. Being a private enterprise meant you could focus on client service instead of shareholder returns.

Dan did all this with an indefatigable work ethic, ready charm, and humility. He nourished relationships and turned clients into lifelong friends. My father was never showy or fancy. He drove his old blue Buick until it gave out, and wore his impeccably tailored suits almost until they were shiny.

While he was proud of his Jewish roots, back in his day, Jews had to be better than others to get ahead. Faith shaped Dan's steadfast belief in ethics. For Dan, there was no gray, only black-and-white. Ethics and a sense of doing things "right" affected everything he did, including his business, where transparency and candor were, to him, of paramount importance.

In business and in pleasure, Dan has always been in it to win it. He loved sports, especially tennis. He was Rafael Nadal long before Nadal was born, running after every ball. To say that Dan was fiercely competitive and attuned to the finest details to gain an edge over an opponent is an understatement. But he took victories in stride and learned from setbacks.

My father's life had a hum to it – like that of steady machine drum churning through information and weaving together random pieces of data or opinions to form a whole piece of cloth. Dan maintained voluminous files on every client or prospect. His desk was stacked high with papers and periodicals – a veritable mad scientist's lab – but he knew where every item was. Dan usually ate lunch at his desk – a sandwich, an apple, and a cookie. But he ate only half of the cookie, because he wanted to maintain the same slim figure for his daily weigh-in. He dictated into a tape machine or wrote longhand with a blue or black felt tip pen. He kept his secretary typing away at the IBM Selectric all day, churning out his famous "Dan-o-Grams," which critiqued work product, prodded the underperforming, or gave encouragement to a lonely son at camp, away from home for the first time.

He regarded public relations as a higher form of communications than advertising because it encouraged dialogue with consumers and relationship building with opinion leaders. His visionary gift was exemplified in his early recognition of the importance of two-way communications, which are now made even more effective through social media. To this day, a signature Edelman campaign has an interactive public service element.

Dan believed that outstanding client service and brave ideas were fundamental to long-term relationships. "Every Edelman person is an account executive on client assignments," he would say. And "It is great to be the biggest P.R. firm, but we must always strive to be the best firm."

But even with all his successes – and setbacks – family mattered most. As I write this, Dan's partnership with his wife and our mother Ruth is close to 60 years old. Hers was a busy life, out most nights, pushing the children to excel in school, managing the summer house in Charlevoix, Michigan, with guests nearly every weekend. To this day, she and Dan hold hands, deeply in love.

Dan has always been fiercely proud of his children. My brother, John, became the founder of Edelman's human resources department, and now serves as the first managing director of the firm's Global Citizenship and Sustainability Initiatives program. My sister, Renée, who shares Dan's love for journalism and attended Columbia Journalism School just as he had, is now a top public relations professional in the firm's technology division. Dan has also been an inspiration to my three daughters, holding them to the same high personal and professional standards demanded of all members of the Edelman family.

My relationship with my father was complicated. He cast a long shadow and expected that I make the most of myself. When I was in my early teens, our tennis matches often resulted in a racquet thrown in frustration as I lost, yet again, to a superior strategist. Only when I began to work at Edelman did I begin to understand his relentless drive for perfection, his sense that success could evaporate unless you tried to do your best every day.

We have been partners in building a great global enterprise, different in our operating styles but identical in our objective. I have called him every day wherever I am to brief him on the business, listening carefully to his advice. In 1996, he told me that he was proud of my achievements and that it was time for me to take over the firm – high praise from the founder of a company and creator of a profession . . . and from a father and a mentor.

There will never be another Dan Edelman – indomitable, ever modest, always resilient, ready for the next challenge. His story inspires us all.

Richard Edelman

CHAPTER 1

THE TOUR BEGINS

On an icy Chicago afternoon in February 1949, Toni Company CEO Neison Harris barged into the office of Dan Edelman, his young public relations manager. Dan could see from his boss's demeanor that something was terribly wrong.

The hard-charging chief executive of the home permanent maker explained that the famous Toni Twins – the company's spokesmodels and stars of its "Which Twin has the Toni?" advertising campaign – had been arrested in Tulsa, Oklahoma, during a publicity tour that Dan had organized. A state board of cosmetology inspector, Enola Shumate, had – following an in-store promotional appearance – thrown them in jail for practicing salon procedures without a license.

Dan's seemingly brilliant idea – a groundbreaking, 20,000-mile, 76-city media tour to boost sales of the No. 1 home permanent kit and stave off fast-encroaching competition – had come to a crashing halt.

"Well, what are you going to do?" demanded Harris.

A MOVE TO CHICAGO

New to the company, the industry, and the city, the lanky and bespectacled Dan had recently asked himself the same question many times.

Six sets of telegenic twins were chosen to travel the country on behalf of the Toni permanent wave kit. In whatever city they landed, the twins would make in-store and media appearances, with one in each set sporting a Toni permanent and the other a salon wave. The tour, the brainchild of 28-year-old Dan Edelman, became known as the first-ever marketing media tour.

Which Twin has the Toni?

(and which has the $15 beauty shop wave? See answer below)

More than 2 million women a month use Toni
...the wave that gives that natural look!

The wave that gives that natural look . . . Toni

A year earlier, he had been an entry-level publicist at Musicraft Records in New York, a jazz label owned by his brother-in-law, Irving Felt. The company's talent roster included well-known entertainers Sarah Vaughan, Duke Ellington, and Dizzy Gillespie. Dan spent his days writing liner notes, schmoozing with D.J.s, and arranging artist appearances.

He also had helped with the production of a 15-minute NBC radio show starring up-and-coming Musicraft crooner Mel Tormé and sponsored by the Toni Company.

"I'd never heard of Toni, but picked up one of their home permanent wave kits," said Dan. "I decided to make up an album of four sides of Tormé recordings and send it to disk jockeys around the country." To draw more interest, Dan packaged the records in a pink-and-white-striped cover made to resemble Toni's packaging. "The disk jockeys played the records and talked about Tormé and Musicraft – and also Toni."

On a muggy summer afternoon, as Dan packed up another batch of albums to send to more D.J.s, Toni television and radio manager Don Paul Nathanson looked on. "Don was kind, gentle, thoughtful, and always considerate," said Dan. "And before the evening was over he offered me a job promoting Toni."

Dan quit Musicraft and became a junior account executive at Edward Gottlieb and Associates, the New York public relations firm handling the Toni campaign.

Later in 1948, Toni decided it wanted someone on the Gottlieb payroll to fill the job of P.R. manager at Toni headquarters in Chicago, and they asked Dan to fill the post. He hesitated, not wanting to leave New York and his network of family and friends. "But since I was the only single man at Gottlieb, I went," he said.

Mel Tormé sang on an NBC radio show sponsored by Toni.

"I said I'd do it for 90 days, but I said I wanted to return and live and work in my hometown, New York." But he didn't return to New York. He quit Gottlieb and went to work directly for Toni.

The 28-year-old Dan struggled early on. For starters, he knew nothing about Chicago, and less about the workings of corporations like Toni and its parent company, Gillette. What's more, he had no experience in consumer sales to women or the beauty market as a whole. The only thing he knew about hair was that he no longer had much of his own.

Dan even had trouble persuading his own mother to support the idea of home permanents. After receiving a Toni kit from her son and declaring it a "great success," Selma Edelman wrote Dan and admitted she had only used the rollers and not the permanent cream – "that is difficult to do oneself." She wondered if "there were any agencies that you can call up, and ask for a girl to come to your house by appointment say for about $2.00 and extra if you want it set."

WHICH TWIN HAS THE TONI?

Thanks to Neison Harris's salesmanship, his brother and co-president Irving's coolheaded financial skills, and a brilliant campaign concept from the advertising agency Foote, Cone, & Belding, by 1949 the Toni Company was selling a third of all home permanents.

Toni was a sponsor of the Miss America Pageant, which gave Dan the opportunity to present a prize to Miss Nebraska.

The campaign, featuring identical twins with identical hairstyles, asked consumers to decide, "Which Twin has the Toni?" Ads explained that one permanent cost $15, the other only $1.25 (later $2.00). "Easy as rolling your hair up in curlers."

The catchy slogan and engaging approach captivated women and rocketed Toni to the top of the home

Walter Winchell, a popular newspaper columnist and radio and television personality in the 1950s, shakes hands with Dan while holding a Toni kit.

permanent market. Neison and Irving cashed out, selling Toni to the Gillette Safety Razor Company for $20.5 million in 1948, but staying on to lead the operation from executive headquarters in Chicago.

But now the Harris brothers, who'd launched the company in 1944 in St. Paul, Minnesota, with just $1,000 and called it Toni in hopes the name would convey style and ease at a reasonable price, faced a problem. They knew that Toni had only a short window of opportunity to stay on top. Once a woman bought the Toni kit – which contained little more than plastic rollers and a low-cost, ammonium thioglycolate cream – she'd need only cream refills. What's more, competitors were beginning to move into the market with cheap alternatives.

MODERN MARKETING PUBLIC RELATIONS IS BORN

Toni needed maximum publicity for its kits, and Dan was determined to come up with creative public relations tactics to boost sales. He knew the future of his job depended on his ability to do something big. Toni was an established brand and it had a well-known advertising campaign, but it begged for something else that would get American housewives talking. Dan needed to create a buzz.

And then it hit him: A media tour.

Politicians and celebrities had long toured America, going from one speaking engagement to the next. What if, Dan thought, a company organized a tour geared not toward events, but aimed at local media? A media tour would ignite conversation everywhere it touched down. They could easily cobble together a reason to be in town, but the real purpose would be to generate coverage in the local newspapers, magazines, and on local radio.

And television. Especially television. Dan knew television would change everything. By January of

Mona Herche would travel in the east, while Frances and Bernadette Hanson, Jacqueline and Alberta Gubin, and Alice and Alva Anderson would head west. A professional stylist would accompany each group.

To give the campaign local raisons d'etre, Dan encouraged media outlets and retailers to organize contests to find a town's most attractive set of twins. And many did. In Florida, the *St. Petersburg Times* launched a beauty contest for twins, while Utahans sponsored "The Misses Salt Lake City," an event at which the win-

The six sets of Toni Twins wave goodbye in front of Chicago's Shedd Aquarium as they prepare to leave for points east and west. They traveled in black Lincoln sedans that hauled pink-and-white-striped campers – caravan style.

1949, the number of TV stations in the U.S. had exploded from a handful to a hundred in 58 cities. Soon, half of all American households would have a TV set. To finance programming, networks turned to corporations, and Americans tuned in to *Kraft Television Theatre, Texaco Star Theater,* and the Lincoln-Mercury-sponsored *Ed Sullivan Show.* Local broadcasters also relied on help from the business community to fill their schedules.

While nothing like it had ever been attempted, Neison and Irving gave Dan the go-ahead for the nationwide tour. They needed to do everything they could to boost kit sales before the market shifted to refills.

So a media tour it was. Two caravans with Toni Twins on board would move out across the country.

Dan rounded up six sets of telegenic twins and hurriedly made plans for them to travel around the United States for six months. Jane and Joyce Willey, Janet and Jane Leigh, and Carita and

ners received wristwatches and the opportunity to join the Toni Twins during their appearances at local department stores.

Dan boosted the hype of the spectacle by insisting that the groups travel in black Lincoln sedans pulling pink-and-white-striped campers with the words "Toni Twin Caravan" painted on their sides. On a sunny winter day, all the twins, bedecked in Ceil Chapman dresses and bundled in Dorothy Esther fur coats, waved to the cameras in front of Chicago's Shedd Aquarium before taking off on their journeys.

From the opening days, there were mixed results. Some cities embraced the well-coiffed women. Others turned up their noses at the "publicity stunt." Dan told his bosses that the success of the tours rested not on crowd size, but on media coverage, and, ultimately, of course, sales numbers. He counseled them to be patient.

Dan caught flak from the twins themselves, too.

Several bristled at the jam-packed schedules. On the eastern tour, the twins staged a sit-down strike in Miami, refusing to continue unless they could spend an afternoon at the beach. Dan gave in, and the motorcade rolled on.

BEHIND BARS

As the tours made their way around the country, American beauticians began to organize in opposition to home permanents. Toni and similar brands had sliced salon revenues by 20 percent, according to trade estimates. So the beauticians began to take action.

Stylists in 35 states hired lobbyists and pressured legislatures to ban home perms or force Toni and other companies to print ominous "poison" warning labels on their kits. Angry Louisiana hairdressers formed Beauticians United, while the Kentucky Hairdressers Association sponsored legislation that threatened incarceration for anyone "operating a beauty shop without a license."

In Tulsa, no one was as perturbed as Enola Shumate, a member of the Oklahoma Board of Cosmetology, the state licensing and regulatory agency. If the industry didn't do something, home permanents would destroy the salon business, she warned. Then, as if on cue, opportunity landed in her lap: Dan's twins were on their way to her home turf.

When the western caravan arrived in Tulsa, the media made a decision not to play along. The *Tulsa Tribune* and *Tulsa World* refused to cover the tour, even though Dan had arranged for the

The western portion of the Toni Twin caravan finds itself in jail after state board of cosmetology inspector Enola Shumate ordered the twins' arrest for practicing salon work without a license. For Dan, the arrest proved a lucky twist. He called the Associated Press, which ran the photo, sparking an avalanche of nationwide press coverage.

women to have photos taken with Mayor Roy Lundy presenting them with keys to the city.

An editorial in the *Tribune* was blunt, refusing even to mention Toni by name. "All the 'which twin has the ___' publicity stunts were falling flat as a flounder. The twins, three sets of them, came to town. But nobody displayed much interest. They whirled around in cars with the trade name painted on the sides, preceded by a shrieking siren. A few people glanced their way. That was all."

Shumate watched the procession and waited until police escorts dropped off the twins for an in-store appearance where they posed for photographs. When the twins concluded their business and headed back to their hotel, she swung into action.

Citing state statutes, Shumate ordered the police to have the twins arrested. All six of them. The accompanying hair stylist, too. Clearly, said Shumate, the group was in defiance of laws prohibiting them from practicing salon work without a license. There were reports that the twins had even touched a customer's hair! The authorities had no choice. Police officers who had escorted the Toni Twins into town now sheepishly led them off to the city jail.

Word spread quickly among Oklahoma beauticians. "Most of the state's beauty parlor operators are frankly, openly, and aggressively fighting all varieties of 'home' beautification of the female," summarized the *Tulsa Tribune*. "Cuts them out of business."

"THIS IS WONDERFUL"

When Neison Harris burst into Dan's office to tell him about the jailed twins, the news caught Dan by surprise. Though he was an obsessive planner, he had never dreamed of this possibility. Dan saw the panic in his boss's eyes. Then he did something that surprised Harris. He smiled.

"This is wonderful," said Dan. "Just wonderful."

Harris didn't understand.

"We call the Associated Press," said Dan. "We tell them the twins have been arrested. There'll be news stories across the country."

Dan gathered as much information as possible from a local Tulsa attorney Toni hired to represent the twins. He then phoned the newswire services to let them know innocent women were being incarcerated in Oklahoma for giving themselves permanent waves. Attractive twins nonetheless. Did they want a photo?

Within hours, stories popped up on radio and in newspapers nationwide. Meanwhile, Oklahoma officials, recognizing a gathering storm of public disapproval, set the twins free. This gave Dan another story to pitch – "Twins Released from Tulsa

Girls across the U.S. played with Toni dolls in the 1950s.

Jail!" Media attention gathered speed, first with the dailies and radio and television reports, then with magazines like *Life* and *Reader's Digest*.

Capitalizing on their brief time behind bars, the twins drew bigger crowds and brighter media spotlights than ever. Mayors, governors, and vice presidential candidates jockeyed to have their photos snapped with the beauties.

An ad for the Toni doll. The toy would become the country's best-selling doll for five years.

ALL THE RAGE

The phenomenon spread. Mothers dressed their children as Toni Twins for Halloween, while movie stars Rosalind Russell and Loretta Young donned Toni Twins costumes for the Hollywood Press Photographers Costume Ball. Women organized Toni clubs and Toni tea parties to help each other with home permanents. By the end of 1949, more than 65 million women had purchased Toni kits.

Toni executives capitalized on the craze. At Dan's suggestion, they allowed the Ideal Novelty and Toy Company to create Toni dolls, hard plastic figurines with nylon locks dyed blonde, brunette, black, or red. The dolls came with rollers and end papers, a plastic comb, and a home permanent solution made from water and sugar, all the implements a little girl would need to groom her toy to look just like Mom. For years, they were the country's best-selling dolls.

In 1950, Americans tuned in to *Toni Twin Time*, a live, 30-minute television variety program featuring singers, dancers, comics, and hostesses (twins, of course) who prompted the audience to guess: "Which Twin has the Toni?" But an uninspired format and excessive commercial tie-ins doomed the show after just half a season. The series would have been buried more deeply in obscurity had it not been for the future exploits of its young host, a then-unknown actor named Jack Lemmon.

The Toni Company had better luck when it signed on to sponsor the *Arthur Godfrey and His Friends* television variety show. Known for promoting only products he admired, Godfrey effortlessly worked Toni into the improvised banter that was his trademark. "It has always been a pleasure presenting Toni to the public," said Godfrey. The show ran through 1959.

Meanwhile, Dan had his hands full with legislative fights across the country. He traveled to state capitals like Baton Rouge to convince legislatures to kill bills intended to harm Toni and the home permanent business. "When the bill was brought up in the Louisiana legislature, a man who was as bald as I am now stood up and said, 'Just look at me. I've been using Toni all my life and see how much good it's done for me.' The bill was laughed out of the legislature," said Dan. The scene repeated itself across the country.

Dan walked the halls of the Toni Company and received kudos from his colleagues. Ever the advocate, he distributed press clip packets and briefed executives on his public relations efforts.

His colleagues would also come to learn that Dan had not only scored a coup for the company, he'd orchestrated the birth of modern marketing public relations. The media tour would become a staple for thousands of product launches in the decades ahead. He had shown the world how to make a consumer brand come alive.

Yet just when Dan cemented his status at the company, everything around him shifted. Sales of the

The Toni Company sponsored the *Arthur Godfrey and His Friends* television variety show, hosted by Godfrey, one of the best-known American television personalities of the 1950s. A masterly commercial pitchman, Godfrey would mention Toni products throughout the broadcast.

First order of business: Conduct opinion surveys about home permanents among customers and dealers. He knew the most effective public relations campaigns should be grounded in research. Then Dan prescribed a campaign that targeted key constituencies through a variety of venues and methods – women's clubs, community open houses, sports leagues, school programs, and product placements in movies and on television shows.

The plan included collateral materials for salesmen, a booklet for consumers, media events, membership in state drug associations, and outreach to the medical community. It contained employee awards, a company newsletter, crisis and shareholder communications, and even tactics to promote the Toni dolls.

Dan's 60-page P.R. plan for the Toni Company – a comprehensive mix of recommendations that included opinion surveys, product placements, and outreach to groups as diverse as sports leagues and hair clubs.

kits began to plateau. The home permanent market became, as anticipated, a refill market. After spending $20 million on "Which Twin has the Toni?" advertising, Gillette pulled the plug on the campaign, thinking that refill customers would not need as much prodding.

A MASTER PLAN

As his media tours ended, Dan sat down and began to outline a comprehensive public relations plan for the company. He'd never done so before, yet the 60-page document he produced would forever change the course of two entities – Toni and Dan himself. "The simplest way to describe a program of public relations is the following," he wrote. "Do good. Tell other people about it."

The program he outlined was decades ahead of its time. The Toni Company agreed to adopt most of it, giving Dan a public relations budget of $500,000, an astronomical sum at the time.

Dan went to work, implementing the public relations plan to support the Toni permanent kits and the new line of products, none of which had the creative punch of the first wave of kits, nor the iconoclastic advertising effort to support them. The newspaper clip packets he so assiduously compiled began to shrink. What had once been Page 1 photos became back-of-the-paper mentions.

He found himself the victim of too much success, too early. He'd taken a simple product and helped turn it into a cultural phenomenon. But if you hit a grand slam in your first at-bat, every future trip to the plate then pales. For Dan Edelman, a what-have-you-done-for-me-lately syndrome began to creep in.

This didn't bother Dan – who thought exclusively in bigger and better – but the idea of being typecast did. He loved public relations but didn't want to spend the rest of his life promoting hair products. He began to stir and to dream. "Even a good thing can get tiresome," he once said.

So Dan did what he often did at times of decision. He wrote to his father. He admitted to being restless and boasted that he could do a better job than Edward Gottlieb and Associates or any other public relations firm out there. What did Selig Edelman think about the idea of Dan opening his own P.R. firm?

"There comes a time when a man must assert himself and demand his proper place; i.e., at the least, the position and endowments which his talents and past performance entitle him to," wrote Selig in the summer of 1951. "I am happy that you feel satisfied with your argument and am confident that excellent results will follow in due course. Just be patient for a little while longer."

The elder Edelman knew opening a business took finesse. Doing so at an inopportune moment could crush a new venture before it began. Selig counseled his son to do everything possible to start his own company with the blessing – and the business – of the Harris brothers. Wait. Prepare.

Dan took his father's advice. He strengthened his relationships within Toni and attempted to better understand the Gillette business, all while keeping an eye open for potential outside accounts. After a year of preparation, Dan made his move. He stepped into Neison Harris's office to tell him the news. "I'm going to open my own business," said Dan.

Without pause, the nail-biting, chain-smoking CEO threw him out.

"You're fired."

DAN EDELMAN'S ADVICE TO ASPIRING P.R. PRACTITIONERS

Throughout his career, Dan would spend time talking to young people interested in working in the field of public relations. The following is a summary of the advice he would give in speeches, lectures, or simply one-on-one over the telephone. In 2000, in honor of Dan's 80th birthday, the family would work with the Public Relations Society Students Association (PRSSA) to create a Daniel J. Edelman Award.

Read. Every day. Devour important books, newspapers, magazines, and blogs.

Learn to write. Well.

Remember the importance of networking.

Volunteer. Do work for a hospital, art or music institution, or a nonprofit organization.

Continue your education throughout your life. Take classes at night.

Keep in shape, exercising regularly.

Be creative. Strive for the big idea. Be realistic, but dare to be different.

Every good answer begins with proper research. Start with penetrating analysis of the problem and objectives.

Work hard. There is no such thing as a shortcut.

Work hard, but don't be a workaholic. Be sure you have a rich and balanced social life.

Love and be loved. That experience keeps refreshing you and helps you to reach even higher levels of achievement.

Have fun.

CHAPTER 2

BYLINES AND BATTLEFIELDS

The household of Selma and Selig Edelman at 1629 49th Street, Borough Park, Brooklyn, embodied the neighborhood's mix of hopefulness and determination, religion and commerce.

Although the community would later become home to one of the largest Orthodox and Hasidic Jewish populations outside Israel, Borough Park in 1920 contained a diverse mix of European immigrants and religions. It was an area of Victorian homes and large families. The recent opening of the West End subway line ushered in a real estate boom and allowed riders to zoom from Coney Island through Borough Park and on to Manhattan for a nickel fare.

Selig's father, Rabbi Abraham Isaac Edelman, had immigrated to Brooklyn from Minsk, a city in the Russian empire, in 1885. The fresh start afforded him the opportunity to save money for three years before sending for his wife, two daughters, and six-year-old son. Abraham preached to his children the importance of hard work and the rewards that would follow.

Selig took the lectures to heart, excelling at academics and eventually graduating Phi Beta Kappa from City College of New York before going on to the New York University School of Law and a productive law practice. He met Selma Pfeiffer, an immigrant from Kalisz, Poland, at a musicale where she played

Dan pictured with his parents Selma and Selig Edelman, in
Brooklyn (top) and in Florida (bottom).
Rabbi Abraham Isaac Edelman, Dan's paternal grandfather
(opposite page).

"Kiss Me Again" and "Samson and Delilah" on the piano. She had studied voice and piano for three years in Berlin and taken a voice coach at the Metropolitan Opera House in New York. Selig walked her home from the show, and married her in 1910.

When asked at their 50th anniversary to describe the home, Selma reflected and used one word – "disciplined." Their sons Morton, Albert, and Daniel, and daughters Elaine and Harriet worked hard, with shortcuts and middling grades unacceptable. The Edelman home was filled with industriousness, but also the comforts of a large family and the notes of Selma's Chopin sonatas. "I wrote some of my best briefs to her music," said Selig.

A BEGINNING IN BROOKLYN

Dan as a baby.

Born July 3, 1920, Daniel J. Edelman may have missed being a Fourth of July baby by hours, but his childhood was nonetheless all-American. Studies filled his days, with any extra time allotted to baseball, synagogue, a *Brooklyn Daily Eagle* paper route, and writing, always writing.

At age 5, Dan contracted the mumps. Quarantined to a guest room, he slipped typewritten notes to his mother, requesting lunch items or more blankets. From that day on, his was a world to document and share. "I have always thought of myself as a journalist," he said decades later.

While close to his three older siblings, Dan forged a special bond with his younger sister, Harriet. He walked her to school each morning, holding her hand and counseling her on the best way to approach the day's tests and challenges. She'd

smile at him with cherubic cheeks and soft blonde waves.

In 1928, with Selig's law practice growing, the family moved to 600 West 111th Street, in the Morningside Heights neighborhood of Manhattan, a stone's throw from the halls of Columbia University. The change of address took the Edelmans away from their filial Brooklyn confines, but transported the kids into a new, exciting world of Riverside Park, the Ivy League, and endless possibility.

That buoyancy was chilled by the stock market crash of 1929. Dan saw former Wall Street traders and besuited businessmen now hawking fruit on street corners. "It was at that time I learned to pick up every penny I saw," said Dan.

For the Edelmans, the Depression meant sacrifice, not ruin. Selig's law firm handled bankruptcy litigation, a growth business. He kept his job and the family's house through the down times.

To 11-year-old Dan, the world needed to know what was going on in his community. He and a neighbor produced a regular news flyer. "A friend and I collaborated in writing and typing it and we made copies on one of those gelatin-type reproduction units in his house," said Dan. "Circulation reached an all-time high of 50 copies."

The only passion challenging Dan's love for writing was his affection for baseball and the Brooklyn Dodgers. Unfortunately, his father didn't share Dan's ardor. On the one afternoon Dan was able to convince his father to take him to Ebbets Field for a game, Selig kept his face buried in the newspapers.

In Manhattan, Dan and Harriet grew even closer. Dan worked with his sister on homework assignments and took her to nearby parks or the latest Charlie Chaplin movie. He helped her create

Harriet and Dan Edelman in the early 1930s. Of his four siblings, Dan was closest to Harriet who in 1934, at age 10, contracted mastoiditis and died.

scrapbooks of current events, binders full of clippings detailing Charles Lindbergh's flights and Mayor Fiorello H. LaGuardia's election. Harriet worshiped Dan and took his counsel to heart. Her perfect grades matched his, subject for subject.

In the winter of 1934, against the warning of his parents, Dan took Harriet to the movies. The dark months had been some of the coldest in memory. In February, temperatures averaged 19.9 degrees, still a record low. A few days after the movie, Harriet came down with a series of headaches and a pulsating soreness in one ear. Not wanting to get Dan in trouble, Harriet hid the symptoms until her parents noticed a growing red bulge behind one ear.

They had seen this red lump on other children before and knew its ominous meaning. Mastoiditis, an inner ear infection that spreads to the skull's mastoid bone, was a leading cause of childhood mortality in the 1930s. Penicillin was still a decade away. Researchers recently had developed the world's first antimicrobial medications, which would soon cut child mastoiditis mortality rates by 60 percent. They would not be available to the public for another year.

The Edelmans reached out to experts to get Harriet immediate care. Oldest son Morton, a student at Johns Hopkins Medical School, queried ear specialist Samuel Crowe, a physician who opened

the nation's first otolaryngology clinic. "Dr. Crowe does not think headaches normal result of mastoid," Morty telegraphed in April. "He thinks it requires immediate attention. He sees chance inflammation departing entirely but would not wait too long."

On May 12, 1934, as New York sprang to life from the brutal winter chill, Harriet Ruth Edelman died. And with her, a piece of Dan Edelman. He would never fully recover.

> Harriet Edelman
> November 15, 1933
> Spelling
> 100
>
> Poetry
> Thank you for the winter days
> Beautiful with ice and snow
> Merry rides in jingling sleigh
> Coasting skating too and fro
> Thanks for joyous Christmas tide
> And the pretty stories told
> By the bright and warm fireside
> Safe from harm and wind and cold

Harriet wrote this poem in her school notebook six months before her untimely death in May 1934.

No one in the Edelman clan took Harriet's death harder than Dan. For the rest of his life he questioned whether he was partially to blame for her demise. Why hadn't he listened to his parents? Why had he he insisted on going to that movie? Reassurances from his family that Harriet could have contracted the infection at school or anywhere did little to assuage his pain and lessen his guilt. With a fractured heart, he soldiered on.

LESSONS, LIFE

After skipping several grades, Dan enrolled at DeWitt Clinton High School in the Bronx, at that time one of the largest high schools in the world. He took three subway trains to get to the campus, where he brushed shoulders with the likes of future journalist Daniel Schorr, *Gilligan's Island* creator Sherwood Schwartz, Cantor Fitzgerald founder Gerald Cantor, Yankee pitcher Ed Lopat, actor Stubby Kaye, attorney William Kunstler, and champion boxer Sugar Ray Robinson.

The long hours and academic trials at DeWitt Clinton gave Dan something to think about other than losing Harriet. Her death propelled him to work harder and be a more obedient son than ever before. He persevered as if carrying on for the two of them.

DeWitt Clinton High School is where Dan learned how to write like a journalist. With the help of friend Jack Raymond, who later covered military affairs for the *New York Times*, Dan secured a spot as sports editor of the *Clinton News*. He savored the assignment, the combination of his two loves – writing and athletics. His storytelling prowess grew with each deadline.

Despite being a couple of years younger than most of his classmates – he graduated at age 15 – Dan decided to run for class president. He attacked the campaign with a combination of Selig Edelman's debating skills, a well-defined message, and a dose of his own hucksterism. It would be his first public relations campaign, and it did not go according to plan.

"I lost by a rather narrow margin," said Dan. "And

As a marshal of the class of 1940, Dan leads the Commencement Day procession at Columbia College. Like his father, Selig, Dan graduated Phi Beta Kappa.

we couldn't figure out why. So we did a little investigation and found a lot of my ballots in the toilet. A typical Tammany Hall-like operation."

Dan never solved the mystery of the stolen ballots. Instead, he came away from the election with a bigger question. "I thought a lot about that incident," he said. "Maybe I would have won and maybe I wouldn't. But it was kind of reflective of this struggle going on within me: Did I want to report the news or make the news."

At age 16, Dan continued this internal debate at nearby Columbia College, just a couple blocks from home. He'd begun to fill out his six-foot-plus frame and lose the childlike puffiness in his cheeks. Dan joined the staff at *The Spectator* newspaper, penning the "Sidelines" sports column and reporting on "Lion dribblers" and the "bright stars of the tank squad."

He found a home at the Zeta Beta Tau fraternity, where he befriended a fellow Brooklynite skilled on the football field yet struggling to make grades – future Chicago Bears star Sid Luckman. As he had with Harriet, Dan tutored the older Luckman. He helped him wash dishes at the fraternity. Their friendship benefited both young men; Luckman raised his grades and helped Dan get elected fraternity president. Two years later, Dan graduated Phi Beta Kappa with honors in history. He was also elected "best politician," a "somewhat questionable honor," joked Dan.

Meanwhile, in Europe, Adolf Hitler's troops continued to overrun sovereign nations. Morton Edelman would soon be off to New Guinea and the Philippines to treat servicemen suffering from tropical diseases. Albert Edelman served as a lieutenant commander in the U.S. Navy. Selig urged his youngest son to hold off on volunteering for service. So, Dan continued on at Columbia, entering the School of Journalism.

THE REAL WORLD

After graduation in 1940, Dan headed north to Poughkeepsie to take a job as a reporter for the *Hudson Valley Sunday Courier*. His entry into the world of professional journalism came courtesy of a Columbia classmate whose family owned the paper.

For a man who'd spent his entire existence in one of the world's most dynamic cities, the move to Poughkeepsie was a reminder the life of a reporter was often far from glamorous. His "One of the People" column highlighted local residents such as a 72-year-old teashop owner, a former vaudeville actor turned elevator operator, and a Chinese laundry owner.

Dan's oldest brother, Morton, in World War II.

On Dan's first day of work, his editor handed him a camera, a classic reporter's Speed Graphic. "I'd never been a photographer before," said Dan. "So I did some exploratory stuff. I went up to Hyde Park and took a picture of President and Mrs. Roosevelt emerging from church with their guest, Princess Juliana, the future queen of the Netherlands. A little girl gave the princess a bouquet.

"I happened to be going down to Manhattan to see my folks, so I dropped off one of the pictures at the *New York Daily News*. It was on the front page the next day with the caption: 'A Princess Bows.'"

Princess Juliana of the Netherlands, alongside President Roosevelt, receives a bouquet from a little girl. Dan snapped this photo on his first day of work as a reporter for the *Hudson Valley Sunday Courier*. It ran in the *New York Daily News*. First lady Eleanor Roosevelt is second from right.

Dan, here in army uniform, enlisted in 1942 after first being rejected for having poor eyesight.

It also ran on the Associated Press wire and turned up in newspapers across the country. "To my great surprise," said Dan, "I received a check for $25." For the first time, he saw that his reporting could have national reach.

IN THE ARMY

Dan wanted out of Poughkeepsie. Every Nazi conquest strengthened his resolve to enlist and join his generation preparing for global war. He hated townspeople asking why an able-bodied adult carried a pen rather than a rifle. His resolve reached its peak on December 7, 1941, as Dan pored through wire reports of the deadly Japanese attack on Pearl Harbor.

Dan headed to the local U.S. Army induction center, where supervisors rejected him due to his 20/400 nearsightedness, an Edelman family trait.

Adolf Hitler and Joseph Goebbels waged a communications campaign using every form of media at their disposal. Pictured here, a propaganda poster featuring an "Aryan" student.

He turned to the Navy and got the same dismissal. Disheartened he dragged himself back to the streets of Poughkeepsie.

Twelve months later, Dan's draft number came up. This time the recruiters ignored his eyesight. They classified him as 1A, immediately available for service, and sent him to basic training. His military higher-ups soon discovered his nearsightedness, but also his experience as a reporter. Dan was assigned to the Army Specialized Training Program as a public relations specialist to counter the onslaught of propaganda spewing from Hitler's mouthpieces.

Nazi Germany's Ministry of Public Enlightenment and Propaganda, headed by failed novelist Joseph Goebbels, enlisted the services of every writer, reporter, and artist it could reach. Hitler and Goebbels aimed Germany's new propaganda machine on groups deemed enemies of the state – Jews, Bolsheviks, Jehovah's Witnesses, Romani, vagrants, homosexuals, and others. They spread lethal lies through all forms of media, fomenting inhuman sentiments that would ultimately spiral out of control and lead to the slaughter of 11 million innocent people.

Hitler and Goebbels then turned their war of words against Germany's weakest neighbors, using every communications vehicle at their disposal to support their military campaigns: newspapers and magazines; fine art and posters featuring "Aryan" children, sinister looking Jews, and the omnipresent swastika; books and speakers' bureaus; comics and radio programs; and Hollywood-style motion pictures, including Leni Riefenstahl's *Triumph of the Will*.

American generals got a taste of Germany's propaganda juggernaut long before combat. Just as they would need battleships and fighter planes to counter Nazi forces, they would require writers, journalists, and public information officers to fight Hitler's words.

President Franklin Roosevelt formed the Office of War Information in an attempt to marshal American communicators – everyone from Walt Disney to Frank Capra, from Norman Corwin and his *This Is War* radio series to Bill Mauldin and his Willie and Joe cartoons. Roosevelt also instructed his generals to bolster their public

Dan, at right, in training at Fort Jackson in South Carolina.

information capabilities internally with a cadre of public information officers.

Dan packed his duffel bag and headed off to language school, first at Clemson University, then at Ohio State. "They thought that they'd invade Spain or France, so they had thousands of us studying those languages at different universities," he said. Dan faced a more immediate concern: During a routine medical exam, doctors discovered he had a congenital heart disease. They recommended he be discharged.

Instead, he carried on, transferring to Fort Jackson in Columbia, South Carolina, where he honed his craft with the Army's 100th Infantry Division. In a letter to his mother he mentioned that he'd come down with a "drip and cough now and

then." "I've seen half a dozen doctors about it . . . and none of them had any good ideas how to stop it." That cough would linger throughout the war and on throughout his life, with doctors finally diagnosing it as acquired bronchiectasis, a permanent destruction of the large airways caused by untreated infections.

OVER THERE

Dan received his marching orders to join the Fifth Mobile Radio Broadcasting Company, training outside London. While crossing the Atlantic, he listened to radio news reports and produced a daily newspaper. The war forced him to redouble his lifetime commitment to keeping a written record of all that surrounded him.

Relationships played a big part in Dan's trajectory. Keiste Janulis, an older classmate from Columbia, convinced his superiors to transfer Dan, first to Paris then Verdun in northeastern France, to help Janulis prepare a nightly analysis of German propaganda. Shortly thereafter, Dan found himself in charge of the entire operation.

"I was lucky," he said. "A guy called me up who was going to move to *Stars and Stripes* [the Army newspaper]. He asked me if I would handle the job of filling out the reports on German propaganda. And I said sure. It worked out well. We did it in France first, then in Germany."

Dan and a crew of German-speaking analysts would work through the night to document the disinformation. "It was fascinating, assessing the German claims that their V-bombs were destroying London and communicating what Goebbels was saying in his *Das Reich* editorials. My report went to general officers all across the front, from General Omar Bradley on down, and to our propaganda people to help them offset the Nazi claims."

The job had its dark moments as well. "You looked at the number of ships being damaged, according to the propaganda. It was a little scary," said Dan. "But this was literally the 'war of words' and it was our mission to convince the enemy to surrender through leaflets, radio, and loudspeaker broadcasts."

To ease his mind, Dan wrote his parents almost every day. His letters reflected a mixture of routine details and respect for the Allied mission, friendships, and his views on the larger military campaigns going on around him. His correspondence also showcased a growing independence and mounting confidence in his communications abilities. (See sidebar: "Excerpts from Dan's Wartime Letters Home," page 31.)

THE AFTERMATH

At the end of the fighting, Dan was transferred to Berlin, where he helped close down German media, while making sure editors and key reporters weren't fervent Nazis. "That process took a few months and then we reactivated German newspapers and radio, as well as the theaters," said Dan. "We started the magazine *Der Spiegel*, which we produced for a while and then turned it over to German ownership." He also helped to poll German attitudes toward the occupation and the Nuremberg trials.

"I'm going down there [to Nuremberg] again this weekend to assist at a press conference which we will hold on the reaction of Germans to the trials to date," he wrote. "I am preparing a great deal of material based on our opinion surveys and interviews with leading German officials and shall have it mimeographed for distribution; and at the same time shall be oriented on all the material so that I can answer any questions the boys may have."

Waves of reporters roamed Germany in search of stories detailing the war's aftermath. Dan loved hanging out with them. They lifted beer steins and swapped stories. "The more I think of it the more I am convinced that I could make a great start by taking a newspaper job starting at Nuremberg," wrote Dan to his father.

To his mother, he wrote about a different affection. "Betty is a very attractive, very sweet, wonderful company, and really good girl . . . ," he wrote. "I also feel that if I go ahead I should get married over here, in the next month or so, so that we come home together and start together. . . . Seriously, what do you think? Well, I can let out my breath now."

Selma and Selig fired off immediate replies directing their son not to marry a woman he met in the Office of War Information, despite Dan's assurances Betty hailed from Brooklyn and "a good and wholesome background," wanted a "kosher home," and "brings out the best in me." Morty, Albie, and Elaine sent missives echoing their parents' concerns. Dan recoiled.

". . . for the first time I was struck by the complete domination by the family to which I am still subject," he replied to them all. "I feel that this lack of individuality, this hesitancy about doing something on your own . . . has hindered us in many respects, and particularly in the matter of getting the boys married."

Dan returned to America alone.

HOME AGAIN

The United States emerged from the war the wealthiest and most promising nation on earth. Back to her shores came shiploads of men and women, weary yet full of hope. While many would struggle with the transition from military missions to desk and factory jobs, most service personnel returned home believing in the country, its future, and the industries that would drive its economy.

Amid the returning soldiers came a corps of communicators, writers, reporters, and public information specialists. Men and women who had matched Nazi propagandists word for word – and won. They reentered the U.S. workforce with razor-sharp skills, ample contacts, and confidence they could influence the masses with good and honest information. They benefited from good timing, as the nation's economy was not only booming, but had started to shift its focus from manufacturing to service industries.

Office of War Information veterans included people like historian Arthur Schlesinger, poet Archibald MacLeish, and journalist James Reston. The war also shaped many of the men who

Dan in Europe during World War II.

would go on to pioneer the field of modern public relations. Army Air Corps Major Alfred Fleishman surveyed the needs of displaced Jews. Harold Burson, a 24-year-old Army engineer, covered the Nuremberg trials for the American Forces Network.

Dan Edelman felt ever the equal among these talented men and women. He developed the chops for a career in communications, though he wasn't sure which direction to take. With the fighting over, Dan revisited his longtime internal debate – should he be a news reporter or a businessman?

Daniel J. Edelman
115 Central Park West, New York, N.Y. (Sc 4-3220)
Age: 26

B.A. Columbia College (1940)--Phi Beta Kappa, Honors in history, member
    Student Board, Van Am and Nacoms societies, fraternity president,
    Dean's advisory board, tennis.
M.S. Columbia Graduate School of Journalism (1941)

From June 1941, Sports Editor Hudson Valley Sunday Courier, in
Poughkeepsie, N.Y., and commentator Radio Station WGYN, covering
Poughkeepsie and Newburgh. From January 1942 reporter Poughkeepsie
New Yorker, daily afternoon newspaper, covering city affairs, and
originator and writer of regular column, "One of the People." From
August to November 1942 served as assistant city editor of the paper.
During time in Poughkeepsie served as stringer for United Press,
covering Poughkeepsie regatta and other special events.

Entered Army in December, 1942, assigned to G-2, 100th Infantry Division,
as publicity man, writing regular releases on division activities and
weekly orientation lecture for all regiments on current affairs. After
specialized training at Ohio State University, assigned to psychological
warfare training at Camp Ritchie, Md. Served in England, France and
Germany with Mobile Radio Broadcasting company assigned to 12th U.S.
Army Group; wrote and edited daily analysis of German propaganda
trends based on monitored radio reports. Appointed chief of monitoring
section, responsible for enemy as well as Allied news report, both of
which were teletyped to all Armies and many individual divisions in
the field. At the end of the war joined the Intelligence section of
the Information Control Division of Military Government for Germany,
which controlled press, radio, theater, motion pictures, etc. in
occupied zone. Originated and wrote a daily intelligence report on
German attitudes toward the occupation, reactions to food quotas,
sabotage, etc. Also served in US Zone as ICD's public relations
officer, releasing stories to US press on division activities and
arranging press conferences. Called to Berlin in February 1946 as
ICD reports officer, writing daily, weekly and monthly reports on
division activities and continuing on public relations. Special
releases included stories on German attitudes to the Nuremberg trials
(based on ICD surveys), which was released in Nuremberg, and on
blacklisting of Nazi-tainted Germans in the information fields.
Awarded Army Commendation Ribbon for this work.

In June 1946 started as senior news writer on the news staff of the
Columbia Broadcasting System, writing an average of five news shows
daily, running five to 15 minutes each. Wrote for Arthur Godfrey,
Bill Leonard, Joe King, Harry Clark, etc.

From October 1946 to present, publicity and sales promotion director
at Musicraft Records Inc. Wrote regular releases for press and disc
jockies on artists and tunes and company affairs. Serviced radio
stations with records for play on the air and record reviewers for
review in their columns. Arranged special promotions for distributors
throughout the country and handled New York area promotions, such as
artist personal appearances in record shops and on radio programs.
Wrote album liners and reviews of new releases.

A copy of Dan's résumé from the 1940s, at which time
Dan was employed by his brother-in-law, Irving Felt, at
Musicraft Records.

"I'd been wondering what your reaction would be to working here for a few years, to build a background that would virtually insure my future position on returning to the States," he had written his dad. "Communications will be wide open, and from what we're doing here now we'll be on the ground floor."

During the war, CBS President William Paley had taken a leave of absence to serve as a colonel in the Office of War Information. CBS was in the middle of an effort to beef up its news division, and Paley scoured the military for talent. He hired the likes of Howard K. Smith and Eric Sevareid. Paley promised qualified military communicators a job when they returned.

Dan took him up on the offer, jumping at the opportunity to pen news items for CBS Radio in New York. He wrote stories for a handful of shows and broadcasters, including Bill Leonard and Arthur Godfrey, both former Navy men.

"Arthur [Godfrey] was good enough to supplement my $75 per week salary with a weekly check for $25, which was a kind and much needed bonus," said Dan. "But I had to wake him up every morning at 6:00 a.m. He used to sleep on a cot in the studio after partying at the Hawaiian Room in the Lexington Hotel near CBS headquarters."

Dan enjoyed the work, seeing it as similar to the news summaries he had compiled in France and Germany. But after a few months, the debate between having a career as a chronicler or an entrepreneur resurfaced inside him. He wanted to stake his claim in the escalating American economy. He left CBS to work for his brother-in-law at Musicraft Records, which was followed by positions at Edward Gottlieb and Associates and, later, the Toni Company in Chicago.

After years of having debated between a career as a news reporter or a newsmaker, Dan decided on a future as a businessman. He knew there would be a market for high-quality communications as the country closed out the 1940s and entered an era of unprecedented growth. Atop this megatrend he could carve a career, establish a home, start a family of his own. It was all there, right there for the taking.

EXCERPTS FROM DAN'S WARTIME LETTERS HOME

"Three years today, and the Germans are asking us what's happened to our quick victory. We're beginning to wonder too . . . "
– December 7, 1944.

"Fact is, everything I've done in the Army usually ends in a trash basket, but then the important thing is just getting it done. [Columbia professor Walter] Pitkin used to tell us that you only write your best stuff after the first million words. I wonder how far I have to go."– December 10, 1944

"It seems now that with the tremendous casualties every letter almost contains the name of some new person, friend of mine or one of the boys, who has been killed."
– December 28, 1944

"I got back [from Paris] to find our armies advancing so rapidly that everyone's pessimism receive a sudden optimistic injection. Today we're on the Rhine near Dusseldorf and by the time you receive this will undoubtedly be over. It may only be a matter of weeks now."
– March 2, 1945

"Today is the second day of Passover . . . I had a chance to be at the fine services and the seder the first night. Perhaps the most ironic touch was that the food and the chairs etc. were carted to the hall by German prisoners . . . they were the object of catcalls from everyone. . . . It was quite a sight, and must have proved to those guys that Adolf didn't accomplish his objective of wiping out World Jewry." – March 30, 1945

"It [Roosevelt's death] must be as great a blow to you at home as it is here. Our first reaction was the most oppressive, that all our privations and all the sacrifices of this war might now go in vain." – April 13, 1945

CHAPTER 3

THE BIRTH OF THE BUSINESS

"Fired?" thought Dan as he walked out of Toni CEO Neison Harris's office.

The word stung. Dan had tried to convince Harris that he could do more for Toni as head of his own public relations firm than he could as an employee. He'd proven himself over the last three years, hadn't he? They'd adopted his comprehensive public relations plan. Why couldn't he implement it as an outside counselor?

The passionate Harris would have none of it. He'd given Dan his first big break in the corporate world. He likened Dan's move to betrayal. Go ahead and start your own firm, kid. Close the door behind you on your way out.

Stunned, Dan carried on with his plans. Forget Toni, he told himself. Toni was only going to be the first step. Daniel J. Edelman and Associates would be a broad-based firm serving companies in the Midwest, then New York, then who knows where?

Yes, dream big. That's the goal, Dan told himself. Build the most successful public relations firm in the country. The world.

Dan shared his plan with his parents. "Again we wish you all the good fortune in building up your own business," wrote Selig. "Men of true worth, integrity of character and high capabilities are rather scarce. . . . The treasure and eminent stature of our country were achieved by the practice of the old-fashioned virtues of industry, honor, and reverence for truth and the cherished ideals of our institutions."

At the turn of the 20th century, public relations started to play a role in the country's expansion westward, in entertainment, and in the growth of industry. P.T. Barnum (see poster at right) used P.R. techniques to convince people that his circus was the "Greatest Show on Earth."

Dan faced a hurdle bigger than the Toni Company's lack of support. With many of the businesses he approached, the question wasn't why they should hire Daniel J. Edelman and Associates, but why they should hire a public relations firm in the first place. Advertising, they understood; public relations, they did not.

A LIVELY HISTORY

Public relations – defined in its most fundamental sense as the practice of helping an individual or group enhance its relationship with the public – has existed since the earliest stages of human history. Every major religion or civilization has advanced in part through information dissemination and storytelling.

Yet it wasn't until the turn of the 20th century that public relations emerged as a key component of business. It did so first in the United States, a country founded on ideas and reliant on public influence and persuasive argument. The young nation sped toward revolution after learning of the Boston Tea Party. Alexander Hamilton, John Jay, and James Madison helped win ratification of the U.S. Constitution by publishing the Federalist Papers, 85 articles they penned for the press.

U.S. President Theodore Roosevelt, pictured here in 1903, used public relations techniques to engage with his constituents, a practice he developed in his days as New York City police commissioner.

Americans moved westward following the tales of Daniel Boone, Johnny Chapman's apples, William Frederick "Buffalo Bill" Cody's cowboy shows, and the riches promised by the completion of the transcontinental railroad with the driving of the "Golden Spike." P.T. Barnum convinced audiences that his traveling circus was the "Greatest Show on Earth." A pioneer of community relations, he invited dignitaries to opening nights and donated a portion of each show's proceeds to local charities.

Public relations tactics grew as the nation raced toward the Industrial Revolution, fueling the growth of manufacturing, utilities, and, especially, the railroads. Rail companies like the Burlington Northern and the Santa Fe enlisted artists, writers, and traveling lecturers to reach out to the public and tell them of the wonders that waited at the end of the line.

Theodore Roosevelt, more than any figure before him, embraced the true definition of public relations, employing it not only as a means of delivering a message but also as an instrument to learn from the constituencies he courted. As New York City police commissioner, Roosevelt invited muckraking journalists to join him on crime raids. To promote the national parks, President Roosevelt hiked Yosemite with John Muir, reporters and photographers in tow. When overzealous aides chained a helpless black bear to a tree during one of his hunting escapades, he rebuffed the gesture and turned the helpless creature into an all-time favorite toy and symbol of his conservation efforts. The teddy bear was born.

Edward Bernays, a nephew of Sigmund Freud, used behavioral psychology techniques to sway public opinion.

AGENCIES EMERGE

In 1900, three Boston newspapermen, V.S. Michaelis, Thomas O. Marvin, and Herbert Small, quit their jobs and opened the first public relations agency in America. They called it The Publicity Bureau. Offering "a general press agent business," the three men compiled a client roster that included Harvard University, MIT, the American Telephone and Telegraph Company, as well as railroads opposing regulatory legislation. The Publicity Bureau closed in 1911, but the concept of the independent public relations agency grew.

A handful of men stepped in to fill the increasing demand for corporate public relations. George Parker, a former press aide to President Grover Cleveland, joined forces with a talented *New York Times* reporter named Ivy Ledbetter Lee to form the P.R. firm of Parker & Lee in 1904. Lee insisted on a straightforward brand of public relations, one that abstained from Barnum-style hype. Following a series of rail accidents, Lee convinced the Pennsylvania Railroad to engage the media. He distributed one of the first press releases of the modern era and escorted reporters on a tour of the accident site. The company received favorable press treatment and several other railroads adopted this more open approach.

As America entered the "Great War" in 1917, the evolution of public relations grew in urgency and scope. President Woodrow Wilson tapped former journalist George Creel to organize an enormous coalition of reporters, scholars, and press agents to encourage Americans to support Liberty Bonds,

while boosting morale at home and abroad. The Committee on Public Information, accused on occasion by Congress of embroidering the truth, published a daily news bulletin for newspapers, produced films, plastered the country with posters, and organized a cadre of 75,000 citizens, known as the "Four Minute Men," to give short (four-minute) pep talks around the country.

After the war, a new breed of public relations practitioner emerged, Edward Bernays chief among them. The nephew of Sigmund Freud, Bernays tapped into the growing field of behavioral psychology to craft campaigns that attempted to sway public opinion rather than just present the facts. His controversial efforts helped establish bacon as an American breakfast staple and persuaded many women to take up smoking by connecting the practice to women's equality. Bernays ushered in the era of media events with the creation of Light's Golden Jubilee to celebrate the 50th anniversary of the light bulb.

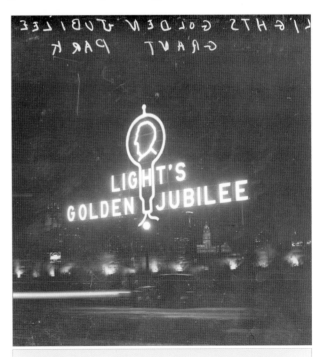

In Chicago in 1929, on behalf of the General Electric Company, Edward Bernays created an extravaganza called Light's Golden Jubilee to commemorate the 50th anniversary of Thomas Edison's invention of the incandescent light bulb.

In peacetime, a host of innovators advanced public relations in multiple directions. Arthur Page, a talented vice president at AT&T, helped establish the practice of corporate communications. Rex Harlow, a Stanford University professor and "the father of public relations research," became one of the first full-time P.R. educators. The top full-service P.R. agencies of the era included Hill & Knowlton, Carl Byoir & Associates, and, later, Selvage & Lee.

Many of America's top public relations practitioners sharpened their techniques as military communications officers during World War II. From the battlefields also emerged a young corps of P.R. specialists who would soon start their own firms; people like Farley Manning (Farley Manning and Associates and, later, Manning, Selvage & Lee), Harold Burson (Burson-Marsteller), Alfred Fleishman (Fleishman-Hillard), John Moynahan (John Moynahan and Company), and Edward Gottlieb (Edward Gottlieb and Associates), Dan's

future employer. Moynahan won a Bronze Star for his work as a communications officer on the Manhattan Project.

When the fighting ceased in 1945 and America got back to business, captains of industry knew public relations would be essential for their companies to thrive. Likewise, small businesses, governments, and nonprofit organizations began to see the benefits as well.

Leading public relations firms in operation before the war, including Hill & Knowlton and Carl Byoir & Associates, maintained their industry edge. Postwar start-up agencies like Burson-Marsteller and Ruder & Finn became top 10 firms within five years.

New and old public relations agencies alike benefited from an economic boom and a host of societal trends. For the first time in the nation's history, most Americans could be reached instantly through telephone, radio, or television. Growth in newspapers and magazines meant an increased need for stories.

To capitalize, P.R. firms offered a full range of services or else they specialized in such niches as entertainment, association work, government affairs, consumer products, or regional public relations. Hill & Knowlton and, later, Burson-Marsteller, took an international approach.

When Americans returned home from the fighting, they came with a little more time, a few more dreams, and a couple extra dollars to spend.

A typical American 1950s family gathers around the television. By the early 1950s it was estimated that half of all American households had a TV set.

For the first period in years, they could focus on themselves, on pursuits like their homes or their educations. Or even their hair.

BUSINESS 101

Dan Edelman couldn't have picked a better time to start a public relations business. Had it been a generation earlier, he would have had a hard time convincing Depression-ravaged companies of the value of outside public relations support. A generation later and he would have joined a crowded field. As would be the case throughout his career, fortune frequently shined on the New York transplant at pivotal times.

An estimated 17,000 men and 2,000 women worked as public relations practitioners in 1950, most as in-house publicists for large companies. They produced corporate newsletters, wrote speeches for executives, promoted products, answered questions from the media, and dabbled in radio and television sponsorships. Department heads also tended to oversee advertising, a field far more lucrative and mature than its adolescent cousin.

Seeing the complementary potential, advertising firms joined the public relations game, adding journalists to their staffs and promising clients "free media" to accompany paid ads. Their longstanding relationships with companies gave them an initial advantage over firms that specialized exclusively in public relations.

Dan Edelman faced these challenges and a host of others, including his minimal experience and lack of contacts. Several competing firms and advertising agencies with P.R. capabilities began operations in Chicago around the same time, including Harshe-Rotman & Druck and Max Cooper and Associates (later GolinHarris).

More than anything, Dan needed to better understand business. To that end, he set out on a mission to meet and learn from as many corporate executives as he could; it was a "crassly commercial outlook," he said jokingly to his father.

"Good education, culture, fine sensibilities play an important role in achieving success and leadership in any particular industry, rather than ruthless aggressiveness and brute force and overreaching," counseled Selig. "So, my boy, continue to 'integrate your social life with business.' At the same time don't neglect the heaven of life, culture, and religion."

Selig and Selma Edelman urged Dan to start his new venture in New York. The comfort and familiarity of his hometown tempted Dan. But he decided that his fledgling enterprise would grow strongest in the soil of Chicago.

Then, a break. A big one. The Harris brothers approached Dan about continuing his public relations work for Toni. After Neison's emotions cooled, the brothers realized that Dan had provided invaluable service to the company. They agreed to pay his new firm approximately $1,500 a month and helped Dan establish a new office near theirs in the Merchandise Mart. No longer would he have to explain their absence from his client roster. The Toni Company was now on board.

ANOTHER NEW ENTERPRISE

In the summer of 1952, Dan spent his days introducing himself to Chicago corporate executives. He spent his nights dating and enjoying the town; his parents remained skeptical.

"Danny darling please be careful when you make your decision on a wife," wrote Selma. "Try to observe, and see her from many angles – to be an interesting person – well you know what I mean. There are lots of things a fellow can afford before he gets married that he must forgo after marriage, if the girl has little to offer – and that sudden change is sometimes very hard for a fellow to take. Just beware, darling, don't get tangled up with anyone less desirable at a weak moment."

Dan met female companions through work, friends, and a thriving Jewish social network. Like most men of his era, he knew he wanted a wife and a family. But that could wait. He had a business to launch, and Chicago was too much fun.

Among the newcomers to town was a recent college graduate from Wisconsin – demure, excited, poor in dollars, rich in attractiveness, with an elegantly arched forehead and long slender arms coppered by the sun. She was a woman whose background differed significantly from Dan's.

Ruth Rozumoff, age 6, left, with her mother, Sonya, and her older sister, Rosalie.

THE ROZUMOFFS OF RACINE

Four-year-old William "Billy" Rozumoff arrived in Racine, Wisconsin, with his parents and three older siblings in 1901, half a world from their famine-racked Ukrainian home of Yelisavetgrad (Elizabethgrad). He assimilated swiftly, breezing through Racine High School, Marquette University, and then Marquette's School of Law. Affable and generous to a fault, Rozumoff built a large-size law practice but struggled with money, often providing his clients with loans and free legal advice. Monetary support to his parents and widowed sister further strained his finances.

Billy married a fellow Jewish immigrant named Sonya Gasul, who had moved to America from Russia in 1916. Sonya and Billy welcomed a baby girl to their brood, Rosalie. A sister, Ruth,

arrived two years later, in 1929. The growing family meant added financial pressures for Rozumoff, who intensified his workload. Without amending his spending and business habits, Billy drifted deeper into debt, depression, and alcohol.

On November 30, 1933, at his mother's house and away from his wife and daughters, Billy died. He was 32. Family members pointed fingers at the bottle and at Billy himself. Either way, his death left a single mother and her two young girls to fend for themselves during America's darkest financial time.

Sonya bundled her struggling family together and carted them off to Kenosha, Wisconsin, where she could rely on the hospitality of her family. Young Sonya knew her options had narrowed. She would marry Max Brill, a divorced man several years her senior, with a family in California he rarely saw. Young Ruthie and Rosalie kept the name Rozumoff and would never view Brill as their father. They later joked that he looked like Nikita Khrushchev.

"As a girl, I dreamed of having a husband, someone who I could love and support," said Ruth. "Someone who could take care of me like my father didn't take care of my mother. I remember I was the only one who wasn't picked up by their father at temple. That hurt. I was about 10. It still affects me. There was an uncle who was good to me. He used to drive me home. But sometimes he wasn't there either."

Hope remained for the daughters of Sonya Brill, but they would have to work hard. Ruth buried herself in her studies and spent weekends clerking in her Uncle Iz's dress store.

An A student, Ruth enrolled at the University of Wisconsin, Madison as an economics major. Her greater goals lay outside the classroom. "My freshman year I had 100 dates!" said Ruth. "I had never dated before college. I just didn't date. I was

hardworking. But I went to college to get a husband. I would have cooking dates. Coffee dates. It was a lot of fun."

Ruth, age 3, in Racine, Wisconsin.

After graduation, she continued her matrimonial quest 140 miles south – in Chicago. She was 21, intuitive, and prettier than ever. College had given Ruth a quiet confidence she could make it on her own, a plan that included a traditional, close-knit family, the kind she'd never known. In the Windy City, Ruth shared cramped apartments with friends and found entry-level work around town, ultimately as a rental agent in a real estate company. She flourished.

Dan and Ruth at the beach in the early 1950s.

"A cousin of a friend came in one day to sign some lease papers," said Ruth. "He saw me and immediately called a coworker of his and said, 'there's a woman here you have to meet.'" The man worked at the Toni Company. The call had been to Dan.

"Dan took me out to dinner, and then we took a ride in his blue Plymouth," she recalled. "We decided to park by Lake Michigan, and I thought, 'uh-oh, I'm in trouble here.'"

But, she needn't have worried. "We talked about hair," said Ruth.

"We talked about Toni. I asked him who should do my hair. He said, 'I'll find out and let you know.' So he called me back the next day and gave me the name of a hairdresser. And I called him back after it was cut because I wanted to keep in touch with him and tell him how the hair was. That was our second date."

After the rendezvous, Dan gave Ruth a dollar for a taxi ride home. She kept it and walked instead.

"I liked him," said Ruth. "I liked him because he was smart, refined, a gentleman, and hardworking. He talked about forming his own business, and I knew he'd be successful. I wanted him from the first day."

Dan had other ideas. The pull of the Chicago dating scene was still tempting. He juggled several relationships, including a serious one with Lois Mell, who would go on to marry Connecticut Senator Abe Ribicoff and enjoy life as a high-profile New York socialite, philanthropist, and fashion doyenne known as Casey Ribicoff.

Ruth was not daunted by Lois Mell or any of Dan's other girlfriends. She opted for a surefire way to his heart: support his plans for the new business. Ruth encouraged his efforts, scurried to meet his work friends, and volunteered to help with logistics.

"This morning I met Norma and we selected three lamps for you," she wrote Dan while he was in New York. "We didn't purchase any, however. The only thing I don't agree on is a lamp on the cocktail table. It will appear cumbersome. I then proceeded to Toni to find Lois Hass. She was ill today so I decided not to see any other of your Toni coworkers."

Ruth flirted and tried to stir his jealousy by hinting of other men. In the end, she always went back to business. "I hope all is crystallizing for you in New York," she wrote. "I'm sure you have captured some and lost some of your sure accounts. I know you will be a success and you must take the bitter with the sweet (this is said in case all didn't materialize). I hope your family is fine and not trying to talk you out of me (wishful thinking)."

Wishful indeed, for Selig and Selma Edelman had begun anew in their attempts to discourage Dan from marrying a woman outside their New York circle.

"Danny dear I desire very much to come and visit with you, but we must avoid long discussions about your girlfriend," wrote Selma. "You know very well how I feel about the matter. I don't see how a fellow like you can be willing to settle in so modest a fashion."

She turned to Selig for reinforcement. He told Dan he'd fly to Chicago immediately to "discuss things more fully and try to arrive at a decision."

"In the case of marriage, the 'sine qua non' for future stability is an initial respect for the girl's personal charms and attributes, her character, her capabilities, her upbringing, and her background,"

The reception area of the first Edelman office, opened in 1952 with a staff of three.

wrote Selig. "Any marked deficiency in these elements which tends to negate that initial respect for one's mate is a danger signal. It's not just a matter of money and furniture."

DANIEL J. EDELMAN AND ASSOCIATES

Daniel J. Edelman and Associates opened for business on October 1, 1952, in a tiny, three-room suite in Chicago's huge Merchandise Mart. The "associates" numbered three.

Chicago offered several advantages, and disadvantages, for new public relations firms. A flourishing economy and expanding media outlets boded well for businessmen like Dan Edelman. Plus, Windy City journalists had the reputation for being more open to public relations than their New York counterparts. On the flip side, Chicago P.R. firms needed to spend more time educating potential clients about the benefits of their services.

Chicago's Merchandise Mart, home to Edelman's first office.

"I remember talking to a company executive in the 1950s who said, 'Give me some of that P and R stuff,'" said Al Golin, chairman of Chicago-based GolinHarris. Golin would have better luck with a cold call he placed to McDonald's founder Ray Kroc in 1957, a public relations account that still continues today.

Dan had trouble connecting with the large, established companies in the area. They preferred to send assignments to the bigger, better-known firms, most with headquarters in New York.

Business order No. 1: Keep Toni happy. Dan knew the immediate future of his firm rested on the shoulders of the Harris brothers. Their name and endorsement would help him immensely in those first few years, the make-or-break period when businesses like his so often failed.

Dan treated the account just as if he'd never left the Toni payroll, dropping by their executive offices daily for planning sessions and informal "hellos." Toni took steps to counter plateauing sales

Dan and Ruth cut the cake at their wedding in September 1953. Ruth's stepfather is seated at left.

and Canada and encouraged local media to hold regional contests. After four months of nationwide press coverage, Toni crowned 21-year-old Marjorie Hightower from Dallas as their queen, and then toured her around the country for several more months of perm publicity, including dozens of television appearances and a screen test with Cascade Pictures in Hollywood.

Aside from Toni, Daniel J. Edelman and Associates' other early clients included a hodgepodge of companies and executives Dan met through the Harris brothers: The American Rack Merchandisers Institute, Holeproof Hosiery of Milwaukee, textile manufacturer S. Stroock and Co., and The Transparent Package Company.

of the original home permanent kits, launching products with differing strengths (Gentle, Regular, and Super) and a Silver Curl line for gray-haired women. Dan and his crew had to get creative to keep Toni products in the media spotlight. He had an idea.

Toni wanted to reach a new generation of customer. Dan's original media tour had been so successful, why not organize another, this time targeting young women? He sold the company on a nationwide beauty contest for college students – the Toni Prom Home Permanent search. He sent entry forms to 2,000 universities in the United States

These new clients didn't want nationwide media tours or sophisticated surveys. They wanted publicity for their niche markets. "That P and R stuff." Dan and his three employees scrambled to give them just that, securing stories trumpeting record sales for the Rack Merchandisers or National Hot Dog Month for the Transparent Package Company, which made casings for "skinless franks."

Early employee Rita Lysen recalled a typical Edelman effort. After the Kinsey Report declared that most American women preferred to sleep in the nude, Dan had a hunch. He sent his staff to Chicago street corners, where they polled women and discovered that in fact, most liked to wear something to bed. Dan sent out a press release on behalf of Holeproof Hosiery. Newspapers ran with the story, "Holeproof President Says Kinsey Is Wrong." Dan's work may not have been as grand as the nationwide Toni campaigns, but the small and growing firm was his own, and that gave Dan immense satisfaction. So did someone else.

THE DANIEL J. EDELMANS

Ruth Rozumoff and Daniel J. Edelman were married in September 1953, in an intimate temple ceremony in Racine. Missing from the 35 guests were Selig and Selma Edelman, still upset that their youngest son had ignored their advice to look elsewhere for a wife. While their absence hurt, Ruth vowed to win them over, just as she had won over Dan.

Months before, she'd taken a break from their relationship to pay a visit to relatives in Miami. Ruth tanned and stayed in shape, wrote Dan cards and hinted about other men. When she returned to Chicago, she called Dan with the excuse of returning his umbrella, a prop she'd kept for just such a purpose. Dan knew the minute he saw her that his parents were wrong.

In the pragmatic world of Daniel Edelman, there was no elaborate wedding proposal, no showy ring or Champagne dinner. Dan and Ruth just decided they'd be wed. They chose Racine to be close to her family. A nearby inn would serve as the honeymoon location.

"We were in a charming little resort in the Wisconsin Dells," recalls Ruth. "And all of a sudden Dan said, 'I have to leave. I have to go with L.C. Murphy of Stroock [Dan's textile client]. She wants me, and I have to go.'"

They packed up Dan's Plymouth and returned to Chicago.

1952 TIME CAPSULE

The year 1952 proved to be an opportune time for the launch of Daniel J. Edelman and Associates, on October 2. The year was auspicious or noteworthy in other circles as well.

Queen Elizabeth II began her reign.

Mother Teresa opened her first Home for the Dying in Calcutta.

At the 24th Academy Awards, Humphrey Bogart won best actor for his role in *The African Queen*, Vivian Leigh won for best actress in *A Streetcar Named Desire*. *An American in Paris* was voted best picture.

Mad magazine and the Mr. Potato Head toy hit the market.

Jonas Salk first tested the polio vaccine he had developed.

The top TV shows in the U.S. were *I Love Lucy*, *Arthur Godfrey's Talent Scouts*, and *Dragnet*.

The best-selling books in the U.S. were *The Old Man and the Sea*, *East of Eden*, *Invisible Man*, and *Charlotte's Web*.

Nearly 60 million people watched Richard Nixon's "Checkers" speech on television.

The Today Show premiered on NBC.

Dwight Eisenhower was elected 34th president of the United States.

Albert Einstein declined the presidency of Israel.

The New York Yankees beat the Brooklyn Dodgers in the World Series.

CHAPTER 4

A RECIPE FOR DISASTER, SUCCESS . . . AND CHEESECAKE

Dan Edelman was growing restless. His two-year-old public relations agency wasn't expanding as fast as he'd hoped, despite the cheerleading letters from his mother. "You are probably the youngest man in P.R. that has started out so big, and that is due to your magnificent background, aside from knowledge of the business, personality, education, good looks, approaching people, I could go on endlessly."

Ruth took a more realistic approach. "I knew it was going to be a slow, hardworking process," she said. "There was plenty of competition out there for him to worry about. But when you're building a new business you have to be optimistic. You have to try hard. You have to do everything to make it go."

After their marriage and abbreviated honeymoon, Ruth moved into Dan's one-room apartment on North Lake Shore Drive. He had a twin bed, so Ruth slept on a pullout couch. "He would come home for dinner around 7:30 and leave early in the morning for work," said Ruth. Two months later, she told Dan that they'd need a bigger apartment. The reason, however, had nothing to do with the sleeping arrangements. She was pregnant. Apparently the honeymoon had been long enough after all.

The newlyweds moved to a three-bedroom apartment on West Aldine Avenue in Chicago's Belmont neighborhood, and Dan intensified his efforts at work.

A selection of stories placed by Daniel J. Edelman and Associates for clients Sara Lee, ReaLemon, and Brunswick.

Dan in a meeting with some of his first employees.

his All-Women Public Relations Firm," joked staffer Rita Lysen.

Dan needed female associates to better understand clients like Holeproof Hosiery and Toni, as well as to pitch new accounts in industries that catered to women. The still-new field of public relations was less of an old boys' network than other service professions. At Edelman and other agencies, doors opened wider for women, minorities, gays, and lesbians, as well as artists and writers who had to struggle in more conservative work environments. Many agency owners embraced this eclectic mix.

Toni continued to be his prime source of income, and Daniel J. Edelman and Associates scored a small victory in 1953 when Toni awarded them their public relations business in New York. That allowed Dan to open an office in his home city and increased the possibility the Edelmans would move back east. Ruth urged him to keep the firm headquartered in Chicago. "I didn't want to go back to his family," she said.

But public relations was still a business, and Dan was frustrated by the slow growth of his. As long as he had Toni, he knew he'd be okay. But he wanted more. He wanted his fledgling firm to join the ranks of industry leaders like Hill & Knowlton and Carl Byoir & Associates. Despite his best networking efforts, Dan couldn't convince Chicago's top business community that his

The strain between Ruth and the senior Edelmans eased on June 15, 1954, the day they all welcomed Richard Winston Edelman to the world. "We had a baby nine months and three weeks after we were married," said Ruth. "After that, everything was fine."

Richard's birth increased Dan's desire for his office to grow. His modest client roster allowed him to pay his rent and maintain a small staff. His hires were young, female, and inexpensive, most with journalism backgrounds. "I called it Daniel J. Edelman and

Dan and Ruth with baby Renée, who joined the family on August 4, 1955.

firm could handle their public relations needs. He worried about being typecast as a boutique firm specializing in women's care products.

An idea to grow and better position his business struck him around the time Ruth announced her second pregnancy, this time with daughter Renée.

MERRIAM FOR MAYOR

Carl Sandberg had dubbed Chicago the City of the Big Shoulders. When it comes to politics, Chicago is also a city of strong arms. Strong, vengeful, threatening arms. To this day, Chicago politics remains a contact sport. Losers rarely emerge unscathed. Through naiveté, blind ambition, overconfidence, or a combination of all three, Dan decided to enter this blood game. He staked the future of his firm on a long-shot alderman running for mayor.

Robert Merriam, a well-educated, North Side politician known as the "WASP prince of Chicago," led a group of reform-minded Democrats opposed to the Cook County Democratic Party machine. Republicans convinced the 36-year-old Merriam, a World War II hero, to run as their candidate in 1955. His challenger mocked Merriam's party switch, joking, "I can't think of anything harder than mating an elephant with a donkey."

To fight his battle with the machine, Merriam enlisted the communications services of Daniel J. Edelman and Associates, a firm led by a man with campaign experience limited to class president elections. This, however, did not give Dan pause. He believed Merriam's

election would propel his firm to the top of Chicago area agencies. He counseled Merriam to hit the Democratic candidate with everything he could muster. With Dan acting as a press secretary, the Merriam campaign accused their opponent of rampant corruption and mob influence.

The target of their repeated attacks: a bareknuckled precinct captain who had fought his way to the top of the Democratic Party hierarchy – Richard J. Daley.

Dan worked his magic with the press, helping Merriam secure the endorsement of the *Chicago Tribune,* the *Sun-Times,* and the *Daily News.* He also encouraged media stories about Daley's attempts

A 1954 press photo of Robert Merriam and family. Merriam's unsuccessful bid to become mayor of Chicago nearly bankrupted Dan Edelman's young company. From then on, Edelman refrained from taking on individual political campaigns.

to buy the election. As proof, the Merriam campaign sent 30,000 letters to registered voters. One in 10 came back as unclaimed or "No One Here by That Name." They estimated that Daley had 100,000 ghost voters on the voting rolls.

Daley also had money. He presided over a million-dollar campaign treasury, three times the size of Merriam's. Daley used the funds to sling mud at Merriam, which included circulating his divorce papers in Roman Catholic neighborhoods and spreading a false rumor that his first wife was black.

Merriam and Dan didn't know what hit them. The final vote tally: Robert Merriam, 581,461; Richard Daley, 708,660. For 22 years Daley would lead the city with a quick fist and long memory. He reminded voters of his electoral strength with a limousine license plate that read "708,660."

For Dan Edelman, the loss reverberated long after Election Day. The Merriam campaign owed his firm an estimated $100,000, money Dan knew he would never see. Worse, Dan realized he'd be frozen out of any city business or corporate accounts close to the new Daley regime.

From that day forward, Daniel J. Edelman and Associates refrained from individual political campaigns.

A PIECE OF CAKE

With the doors to City Hall closed to him, Dan Edelman sought others ajar. He found them at 320 South Plymouth Court, in the exclusive confines of The Standard Club, a storied men's organization founded by German Jews who had been barred from joining other establishments in town after the Civil War. Over paddleball matches and leisurely lunches, Dan befriended many of the area's most prominent businessmen.

Around this time, Dan pitched his services to Charlie Lubin, a high school dropout who opened a small baking company in 1949, naming it after his daughter, Sara Lee. Lubin defied industry standards by loading his cheesecakes with extra eggs and real butter. He charged 79 cents for his

high-quality dessert, twice as much as the competition. When asked why, he shrugged and said, "I like butter myself." Chicagoans agreed, and Lubin's cheesecakes became the talk of the town.

From the beginning, Lubin wanted Sara Lee to expand into a national company, but he didn't have the capital for an expensive advertising effort. When Dan suggested an aggressive public relations campaign for a fraction of the price, Lubin signed him up. Quality, he counseled Dan, that's what separated Sara Lee from its competitors. That's where Dan and his team should focus their efforts.

"There couldn't have been a more cooperative client," said Dan. "Lubin was always ready to give an interview."

Within several months after being hired, Dan and his team secured a *Wall Street Journal* story headlined: "Sara Lee Builds Baking Bonanza on Heaping Slices of Quality." Overnight, the small bakery was besieged with orders from as

"There couldn't have been a more cooperative client," said Dan about Sara Lee, whose founder, Charlie Lubin, agreed to Dan's suggestion to put his limited start-up capital into public relations, not advertising.

The Edelman team earned major publicity for Sara Lee, including stories in *The Wall Street Journal* and trade publications like *Bakers Weekly*. Dan saw the connection between publicity and product sales.

far away as Stop & Shop in Boston and Safeway in Oakland, California.

Lubin cheered the publicity, but worried his cheesecakes and pound cakes would suffer in quality during shipping. After receiving a large order from Texas, he devised a method to bake, freeze, transport, and sell cakes in the same, light-weight aluminum pan in which they had always been sold. Skepticism caused sales to drop by 20 percent in the first months that followed. Once customers tried the frozen cakes, however, revenues rebounded and soon surpassed Lubin's rosiest expectations. The rest of the industry followed suit.

While Charlie Lubin developed a new way to transport food, Dan and his team helped create a new industry model for publicity work, one that stressed direct participation with the CEO and a company's sales force. "Corporate P.R. directors in those days never even spoke to the sales department or the advertising," said Dan. "They didn't think that the work they did had to contribute to sales of the product."

While positive articles in national publications boosted a company's image among the general public, Dan believed industry trade publications were equally important. In the case of Sara Lee, that meant reaching out to media that catered to supermarkets, distributors, bakers, and wholesale purchasers. The sales team would see immediate returns after publicity like the *Bakers Weekly* editorial headed, "The Product that Keeps Its Promise."

The Edelman agency continued to target Sara Lee consumers, too. It got creative. For a food editors' conference in Chicago, Edelman organized a theatrical performance that told the Sara Lee story though a professional play. In another effort, they bused 150 editors to nearby Deerfield, Illinois, for a tour of the new Sara Lee plant.

Dan clicked with Charlie Lubin, a kindred soul who, according to Dan, "dedicated 24 hours a day to his idea and his conviction to make that idea work." Lubin sold the company to Consolidated Foods for $2.8 million in 1956. The self-proclaimed "little old baker" stayed on as president for another eight years, with Daniel J. Edelman providing public relations support right alongside.

"Public relations was worth 100 times the advertising in establishing the success of Sara Lee," said Lubin.

BITTER WITH THE SWEET

The experience with Sara Lee helped position Dan and his firm as an agency of choice for consumer marketing public relations in Chicago. Area executives with products ready for market began calling.

Irvin Swartzberg, a diminutive former advertising salesman, complained about his physician's orders that he drink hot water and lemon juice every morning. The concoction, he didn't mind. It

Irvin Swartzberg developed ReaLemon and turned to Dan for P.R. help. The men befriended each other at The Standard Club in Chicago, where Dan cultivated many successful business relationships.

was the daily chore of squeezing lemons he could do without. Swartzberg suspected many consumers felt the same.

So he began bottling lemon juice in his basement and selling it to Chicago retailers and bars. The early batches were highly perishable and uneven in quality. After several years of experimentation, Swartzberg discovered he could manufacture a consistent, high-quality product by first concentrating the juice, then adding water and a few preservatives. He called the concoction ReaLemon. He'd changed the product, now he needed to change conventional wisdom. After befriending Dan at The Standard Club, he asked him for some P.R. help.

The Edelman agency wanted to stress the product's natural attributes – cost, ease, consistency, and shelf life. First they tackled food recipes involving lemon juice, which had long called for "the juice of a lemon" in their preparation. The agency reached out to food editors, cookbook publishers, home economists, and consumers, letting them know that a few tablespoons of ReaLemon would suffice for the juice of a whole lemon.

They organized television appearances for celebrity chefs who would whip up dishes and desserts using ReaLemon. They sent homemakers booklets with ReaLemon recipes. On press tours, they had Swartzberg tout the product as the answer to a host of kitchen conundrums, including how to keep fish fresh, fruits crisp, and rice white and fluffy.

In 1962, after years of record growth and a near 100 percent saturation at grocery stores across the U.S., Swartzberg sold ReaLemon to Borden, Inc. The new Borden president credited public relations as "a major factor in the increased consumer acceptance of the product."

Swartzberg went on to make not one but two additional fortunes, first as the owner of Mogen

David kosher wine, which he eventually sold to Coca-Cola, and later as the country's first independent distributor of Toyota trucks and cars.

ON A ROLL

In 1937, an inventor named Fred Schmidt, working in a henhouse on a friend's turkey farm, developed a device that would revolutionize a popular American pastime: bowling. The contraption used vacuum power to retrieve scattered bowling pins before rearranging them back into their triangle formation. Schmidt's invention would spell the end of the pin boy, a bowling alley staple. It also threatened the demise of the sport's premier company, Brunswick.

Brunswick, the premier bowling equipment company, hired Edelman in 1956 after a massive loss of business sparked an internal reorganization. During Brunswick's relationship with Edelman, the sport's image changed into one of wholesome family fun.

Schmidt joined up with Brunswick sales manager Robert E. Kennedy, and the pair took the invention to company executives. Brunswick turned them down, preferring to stick with pin boys.

Kennedy then offered the patent to Brunswick's top competitor, AMF (American Machine and Foundry), which saw the device as a surefire way to topple the industry leader. Not only did AMF snap up the machine, it hired Kennedy; and, in 1946, it began to automate its bowling alleys with the mechanical pinsetter. Bowlers shifted to AMF lanes in droves.

Brunswick finally took action, firing chief executive Robert Bensinger in 1954 and replacing him with his brother, Ted. The younger Bensinger scrambled to develop a pinsetting machine of its

own, diverting money from other divisions and borrowing heavily from banks. When the company was ready with its pinsetter in 1956, Bensinger hired Daniel J. Edelman and Associates to spread the word that Brunswick was back in business.

Dan and his crew devised a host of story ideas to fit the needs of key publications and electronic media outlets. For *Fortune*, they outlined six business story lines and opened Brunswick's financial records for the magazine's reporter. Associated Press columnist Sam Dawson was given a scoop that bowling had passed the billion-dollar revenue mark. Edelman pitched *The Wall Street Journal* on a story about Brunswick's thriving school furniture business. *The New York Times* took Edelman's suggestion for a profile on the charismatic Bensinger.

Edelman's media pitches grew more refined each year. Dan drilled his employees on the importance of understanding the needs of each media outlet, learning the tastes of individual reporters, then giving them stories they could use. The results paid off for Brunswick, which passed AMF in pinsetter sales and regained its top industry perch. The Edelman effort also helped modernize and expand the image of bowling from a seedy, somewhat gritty activity to a wholesome, family-oriented pastime.

DEC 1958

Dan's mother, Selma Edelman, with her grandchildren.

HOME, GROWN

The Edelman home roster grew as well. Baby brother John Edelman was born in 1958, making the Edelman family complete. When she wasn't ferrying the kids to nursery school, Ruth volunteered around town, joining a hospital auxiliary board and the Infant Welfare Group. She wanted to contribute to the community, but she also wanted to meet people. She knew networking was essential for a start-up business and for a young couple with no other family in town. She wanted to help.

Ruth and Dan had the idea to host cocktail parties at the Edelman apartment. They were small gatherings at first; just a few clients and journalists, nothing formal. Over the years, however, the parties would expand in size and renown, becoming an indispensable component of Daniel J. Edelman and Associates. They also helped educate Chicago on the possibilities of public relations.

"The way I was most useful to him is that I loved to entertain," said Ruth. "I entertained all the time in grand style. I was known as the Perle Mesta of Chicago. People who came to our house knew they were getting wonderful food and would meet interesting people. I would introduce CEOs to social people. I would mix it up."

With the family, and the parties, expanding, the Edelmans needed more space. Ruth found a nearby apartment that had once been the home of Ellen Borden Stevenson, Adlai Stevenson's wife. But Ruth ran into a problem. The building

Richard, John, and Renée in the 1960s.

had a long-standing tradition of not renting to Jewish or minority families, a common situation at the time. Ruth made the necessary calls and moved the family in. "I had the guts to do it," she said. Life in the Edelman household remained close-knit and optimistic.

With Dan frequently on the road, Ruth lined up schools and afternoon activities for the children. On weekends the family visited museums, walked over to the shores of Lake Michigan, a block away, or organized impromptu baseball games with Richie imitating Mickey Mantle and Renée acting as Yogi Berra.

"I remember Dad always being shaved and wearing a tie," said John. "He told me, 'You never know when you'll need to go in to the office.'"

A child of the Depression, a son of strict but loving parents, a product of academically rigorous schools and the U.S. Army, a man who had never enjoyed an extended vacation or period of rest – all these influences now shaped Dan Edelman, his family, and his firm.

In Dan's mind, he and Ruth and the kids were all underdogs. Deserving, but underdogs. They had to work harder to get ahead. This meant faithful routines, blunt honesty, and unwavering ethics. When you spoke, you spoke straight and true, the same public relations counsel he gave his clients.

"He was very honest and direct," said John. "But he rarely raised his voice. He would say, 'I think you can do better.'"

"One word that I think about when I think about Dan is 'integrity,'" said Ruth. "That's one of the big reasons the company began to succeed. It carried his desire for total integrity."

STANDING UP FOR STANDARDS

While Dan set ethical standards for his firm, he often found himself answering comments about

Ruth and Dan (standing), with Richard in front, are joined by Dan's parents, Selma and Selig. Renée stands by her grandmother and John with his grandfather. Circa 1960.

questionable public relations practices elsewhere. Without a governing body similar to those overseeing professional service fields, like accounting or law, public relations had always been a bit of a free-for-all. As the field grew exponentially after the war, Americans saw the best and worst of the trade.

In Guatemala, operating covertly on behalf of client United Fruit, Edward Bernays launched a public relations smear campaign against the country's democratically elected president, Arbenz Guzmán. Bernays disseminated a stream of harmful information about Guzman to American media, labeling him a dangerous communist. This hardened American opinion against Guzmán and set the stage for a CIA-sponsored coup to oust him.

In another high-profile case, Carl Byoir and Associates organized several third-party front groups for a client, the Eastern Railroads Presidents Conference. The railroad-funded groups spread malicious information about the harmful impact of increased trucking. Their efforts led to the veto of legislation to lift restrictions on trucks. It also led to numerous lawsuits against the railroads and Byoir for using false fronts.

Dan often found himself on the defensive when a company or public relations agency acted in a less than ethical manner. He knew the worst offenders threatened not just his agency, but also the practice as a whole. If public relations was going to succeed, industry leaders needed to stand up for standards. Front groups were a particular affront. Dan had had personal experience. "When I was working for the Toni Company at the Gottlieb agency in New York, I was aggravated that the man who ran the office used letterhead for releases about Toni Home Permanents that read: 'Home Beauty Institute,'" said Dan. "I considered it a clear effort to obfuscate the facts and to present our client as running an institute which of course didn't exist."

"I didn't have the authority at that time to make a change," Dan continued. "But as soon as I became the company's public relations director, I ordered new letterhead that showed that our material originated with the public relations department of the Toni Company. We've aspired to complete transparency."

Dan took his plea to the Public Relations Society of America, the industry's voluntary association. Founded in 1947 as a way to promote standards and education, the PRSA adopted a code of ethics in 1950. At the urging of Dan and other industry leaders, the code was strengthened in 1959 with enforcement provisions and a judicial review process. That, coupled with the public's negative reaction to the Byoir incident and others like it, led to a decrease in the use of front groups and other questionable practices.

Dan's accreditation from the Public Relations Society of America. Throughout his career, Dan called for practitioners to adhere to the group's code of ethics and their own sense of morality.

"We have the PRSA code, and that's a good starting point," said Dan. "But all of us in P.R. must bring to the office our own sense of morality and live by it every day. Let's not allow greed, our drive for success at any price, to undermine the gains we've made. We need to maintain and achieve greater respect." This would be a mantra throughout his career.

Joining Dan in his effort to elevate industry standards was a red-headed sprite of woman named Betsy Ann Plank. Dan hired the Alabama native in 1960. She was a natural, taking up the causes of her clients as well as the industry banner as a whole. Plank would go on to serve as the first female president of the PRSA and help establish a sister association for public relations students. In Plank, Dan found a colleague who would stand up for the profession, even if it meant offending violators.

Moving into the 1960s, Daniel J. Edelman and Associates was on a roll. The Toni account continued

Betsy Ann Plank with Henry Loomis, then director of the Voice of America. Dan hired Betsy in 1960; she would stay with the firm until 1973.

to grow. Sara Lee, ReaLemon, and Brunswick solidified the firm's reputation as the go-to public relations firm for product publicity. The client roster grew to 25, with bigger accounts knocking at the door. Dan also felt encouraged about his efforts to improve the profession. He looked forward to a prosperous decade ahead.

All that changed one morning.

"We had a pretty small operation, maybe 20 people," he said. "I came in one day and there was a note signed by seven of our staff that they had left and had set up their own office across the street. Obviously they'd been planning this for months, because they had the office all set up. Our files were missing."

Dan looked at Betsy Plank and the remaining staffers. How would they survive?

DAN THE GIVER

When we were growing up, my father always referred to the three legs of a stool: work, exercise, and community. They were, he said, the key to a productive life. If any leg became unbalanced, you would fall.

He has given back as a parent, a professional, and as a citizen of Chicago, the city in which he has lived throughout his adult life. When I was at Phillips Exeter Academy in New Hampshire, I once came down with a high fever and strep throat and woke up the next morning to see my father sitting on the edge of my infirmary bed anxiously looking at me, asking how I felt. He had flown to Boston the night before, rented a car, and driven up to be at my bedside when I awoke.

Giving back was part of my father's daily routine. His door was always open and he always answered his own phone, taking calls from civic leaders, clients, prospects, employees, salesmen, and young people just starting out.

When my father was turning 80, I had the idea to have a Chicago street named after him. This seemed a fitting way to recognize the many ways in which he had supported the city. So I went to Alderman Burt Natarus, who knew and respected Dad. He was happy to work out the necessary approvals. He told me that it was important for the city to honor benefactors while they were alive so that they could enjoy the recognition. Honorary Dan Edelman Way is located at the southeast corner of St. Clair and Ontario Streets, near where Dad founded the company.

As managing director of global engagement and corporate responsibility for Edelman, I am proud to be able to build on my father's lifelong commitment to giving.

John Edelman

CHAPTER 5

OPPORTUNITY UNCORKED

When Dan walked into his Merchandise Mart office and discovered that a third of his staff had left to form their own competing firm, he went into damage control mode. Did they plan to take Edelman business with them? How would he provide quality service with a diminished staff? He paused for a moment, then addressed the problem the only way he knew how. Head on.

Dan quickly made plans to get in touch with all of his clients. He didn't want them to hear the news from anyone else, especially a competing firm. He prayed his record and personal relationships would save him. "I visited every single client and told them what had happened," said Dan. "I told them I was their account manager. We didn't lose a single client."

With the crisis temporarily averted, Dan scrambled to hire more staff. He sought strong writers, preferably with journalism experience on daily newspapers. "Intelligence, writing ability, an attractive personality, a willingness to work, and a positive and enthusiastic 'sure-we-can-do-it' attitude," said Dan.

The new roster included people like Judith Rich, a creative marketing P.R. executive, and Harvey Posert, manager of the New York office and a former reporter for *The Commercial Appeal* in Memphis.

Even with the new staff, Dan felt uneasy. The defection made him realize the

Dan with his employees in the firm's early days.

tenuous nature of the public relations business. He understood that his firm was only as strong and as loyal as the people he hired. The incident also strengthened his resolve to diversify, to look for clients in fields outside consumer products and in locations beyond Chicago.

A solution lay 4,500 miles to the east, in the verdant forests of Finland.

"FINNFACTS"

Finland had suffered a series of crushing blows following World War II, having been forced to pay $300 million in reparations and ceding the eastern province of Karelia, a tenth of its territory, to the Soviet Union. The resilient country that had stopped Soviet advances and remained an independent democracy now found itself in a precarious position. It had signed pacts with both the Soviet Union and the West, which prompted many to believe the country was a Soviet satellite. American businesses still looked at Finland with a wary eye.

Frustrated with lingering Western misperceptions about his country, Veikko Konttinen, a communications director for the Finnish Forest Industries Association, had a simple yet radical idea. He would tell the world what was really going on in Finland in the form of a practical, business-oriented newsletter. He'd give the West the facts. "Finnfacts."

Konttinen obtained a small amount of funding from the big timber companies, enlisted the services of a colleague, and formed the Finnfacts Institute in 1960. He had no problem

gathering useful information, but he had no idea how to disseminate it in America and the rest of the free world. The new organization couldn't afford a large public relations agency in the U.S., so it took a chance on a young, Chicago-based firm with solid media credentials.

Dan was delighted. "Finnfacts" was perfect. It would give his firm its first foray into the emerging practice of public affairs. Edelman helped manage brands and products. Now it would manage issues.

The account also got Dan thinking about a branch in Washington, D.C., and rekindled his dream to open a series of offices throughout Europe. "Finnfacts" wanted to start in the United States, but talked about spreading the program to other countries.

The "Finnfacts" account would require Dan and his staff to reach a new circle of journalists – editorial boards, foreign correspondents, political reporters. It also forced the agency to expand its

Dan speaking at Finnish Trade Day luncheon in March 1978 after being presented with the Order of the Lion of Finland by Jaakko Iloniemi, the Finnish ambassador to the United States.

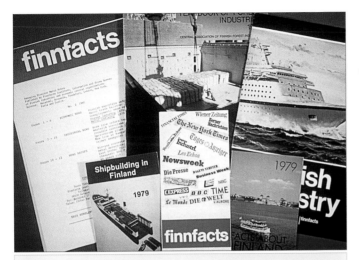

Eight times a year, Edelman produced "Finnfacts," a business-oriented newsletter designed to bolster Finland's economic image in the West.

contacts with policy makers, think tanks, and business trade associations. The new approach and challenges gave Dan and the office a hopeful energy – as well as a healthy fear of failure. This was his chance to help erase the marketing P.R. stereotype. He did not want to disappoint.

From the outset, Dan and his coworkers understood that public perceptions about a foreign country would take longer to change than public attitudes about household products. This would not be a quick-hit campaign. They started by gathering positive stories about the Finnish economy, beginning with core industries like forestry and mining, then moving to specialized brands like Marimekko fabrics and Arabia tableware and the accomplishments of famous Finns like composer Jean Sibelius and architect Alvar Aalto.

Edelman produced the "Finnfacts" newsletter eight times a year and distributed it widely. The firm arranged for American journalists to visit Finland and made Finnish officials available as sources for news stories. When prominent Finnish businessmen and politicians traveled to the U.S., Edelman helped pack their schedules with meetings with American elected officials and thought leaders. The overarching message:

Finland was independent, democratic, prospering, and open for business.

"Our responsibility, then, is to communicate to the media and all relevant publics the true story on Finland and Finnish marketing, business, and commerce, and to engender greater interest in importing industrial and consumer products from Finland," said Dan to a delegation of Finnish business leaders.

Daniel J. Edelman and Associates would tell this story for the next 18 years, during which time Finland grew from a poor, largely agrarian economy into a highly industrialized, modern country with per-capita productivity on par with the wealthiest European states. For his efforts on behalf of the Nordic nation, Dan was knighted and presented with the Order of the Lion of Finland by Ambassador Jaakko Iloniemi in 1978.

Great Britain's Princess Anne, 21, strikes a pose in a Marimekko dress. The popular Finnish brand was one of several that Edelman promoted in its campaign for Finland.

DOWN THE DRAIN

Meanwhile, the future knight faced another revolt, this one led by his seven-year-old son, Richard. "I was watching TV on a Friday night and I saw an Ad Council public service spot that spoofed the Marlboro Man," said Richard. "It showed him sauntering into a Wild West bar, ordering a drink, then collapsing in a coughing fit."

Terrified, Richard took action. He rounded up his father's cigarette packs and promptly flushed them down the toilet. Like many veterans, Dan had picked up the smoking habit during the war, puffing Army-issued cigarettes to stay alert during all-night work sessions. It was a rare vice.

Richard felt satisfied . . . until the cigarettes clogged the toilet and sewage water began to spill out onto the bathroom floor. The Edelmans called a plumber. When Dan bought more cigarettes, Richard clogged the toilet with them again. After the third time, the plumber gave Dan some advice. "He told my dad, 'Look, I'm sick of coming here,'" said Richard. "'Either stop smoking or get rid of your kid.'"

Dan swore off cigarettes.

"He was always very disciplined in his eating," said John Edelman. "And his exercise."

"He lectured us on the importance of the three legs to the stool: your work, your exercise, and your community," said Renée.

Dan and Richard, circa 1963.

In many ways, the Dan Edelman household functioned like a family of recent immigrants – ever-striving, with a strong work ethic and sense of urgency, resources, and expectations heaped upon the children. This began each day at the breakfast table, where Dan would consume *The Chicago Tribune, The Chicago Sun-Times, The New York Times,* and *The Wall Street Journal,* circling articles to give to colleagues, clients, or his kids. The hunger for information rubbed off on the children.

"I would get up early, and run downstairs in my skivvies, and grab the newspapers," said Richard. "But we had to have them refolded and at my father's place at the breakfast table before he came down at 7:30. As long as we had them back in place, we'd be fine."

In word and deed, Dan stressed the importance of maximizing each day and never growing complacent. Don't get hung up on the ups or the downs, the important thing is to do your best, always do your best, he counseled.

In classrooms and athletic contests, Dan told his children, competition sharpens your skills, even when you lose. If you falter, try again. At the family's Charlevoix, Michigan, summer house, Dan once tried to teach John how to ride a bicycle. Dan jumped on a bike and peddled away. Within minutes, he hit a bump and flew over the handlebars, shattering his glasses and carving a deep gash in his face. With blood streaming down his nose and onto his shirt, Dan picked up the bike and continued the lesson.

He showed the same determination at work, where he took copious notes at every meeting and made staff do the same. He sent missives to staff about their performance. The so-called "Dan-o-Grams" were sometimes praiseful, sometimes cutting, but always direct. Staffers knew where they stood. Dan instructed the men to wear suits and ties, and the women to don business skirts or dresses. He always had a comment handy for any employee he saw with unkempt hair or a slovenly appearance.

When Edelman won a big account, Dan didn't buy Champagne dinners or company boxes at the theater. He wore Brooks Brothers suits until they became threadbare and drove cars until they had well over 100,000 miles on them. The child of the Depression avoided debt at all costs, even if it slowed the firm's expansion. He grew his business from retained earnings and kept his own salary to a minimum.

The Edelman children would ride their bikes around Charlevoix, Michigan, where the family spent summers. Left to right: John, Renée, and Richard in the mid-1960s.

PLEASE, GOD, DON'T LET THIS HAPPEN AGAIN

His children witnessed the industrious Edelman approach and adopted it for their own lives. Ruth made sure the kids focused on their schoolwork, hiring tutors and coaches when they needed extra help. The kids accompanied their father to work on Saturdays, entertaining themselves with impromptu games of soccer or hockey in the halls of the Merchandise Mart. On Sundays, Dan and Ruth took their children to Temple Sholom. Though Dan had been raised in an Orthodox home, he switched to Reform Judaism as an adult.

The Edelmans' weekend routines took an ominous turn one winter morning during a family outing. Young Renée complained of being bitterly cold. Her shivers and fever continued for days. A trip to the doctor's office confirmed their worst fears: Renée had contracted rheumatic fever.

Dan and Ruth kiss goodbye in front of the Edelman house in Charlevoix as Dan prepares to return to his workweek in Chicago.

Dan makes a toast to California wines. With no experience in marketing wine, Edelman won the Wine Institute business, which helped the firm open new offices in San Francisco and Los Angeles.

A TOAST TO CALIFORNIA WINES

In the mid-1960s, having finally shaken off the effects of Prohibition and the vine-destroying phylloxera, California wineries began to come into their own. A new wave of winemakers, including Robert Mondavi and Joseph and Alice Heitz, opened for business. They aimed at producing premier varietals on par with Europe's finest.

Most Americans didn't believe it possible. California wineries were best known for their sweet and inexpensive table wines, jug wines, and fortified wines like Thunderbird and Ripple. By 1965, the Wine Institute, the vintners' trade association, decided the industry needed an image overhaul. They fired their three public relations agencies and invited firms across the country to come up with a new communications plan. More than 50 responded with bids.

Daniel J. Edelman and Associates had no experience marketing wine and no offices west of Chicago. Nevertheless, Dan felt he could win the account if he could just meet with the top California winemakers face to face. As luck would have it, the Wine Institute preferred an agency that would leave the wine expertise to them.

Board member Harry Serlis of Schenley Spirits and Roma Wines led the search. He liked Dan's direct approach and low fee structure. After several rounds of screening, he allowed Dan to make a presentation to the board. "I sold that program personally," said Dan. "Without cards. Without film. Without anything."

Dan promised the group large amounts of media coverage, but he also talked about the importance of reaching out to the medical community to stress the benefits of wine drinking. Stories about quality wines and the benefits of moderate consumption would help the California wine

The diagnosis took Dan back to that winter's day when he took his sister Harriet to the movies, then watched her slip away from mastoiditis. Had he foolishly risked another life? Was history repeating itself?

Dan and Ruth found the best doctors and optimal treatments for their daughter. Doctors advised that Renée be kept in isolation in her room, with only occasional visits from family and care providers. The family agonized and prayed. Please, God, don't let this happen again.

After a grueling year, their appeals were answered when Renée regained her health. Dan could turn his attention back to his firm and a new golden opportunity on the West Coast.

industry shake its somewhat lowbrow reputation. They agreed.

Dan also convinced the Wine Institute to fund an African-American outreach campaign, something Edelman was advising for a growing number of clients. Dan's office was one of the first big P.R. firms to establish minority communications capabilities, with staff and resources in Chicago and later in all the offices. He wanted his public relations campaigns to have an impact on as many people as possible.

The Wine Institute business offered numerous opportunities for Edelman to grow. With the account in hand, Dan opened offices in San Francisco and Los Angeles, moving Harvey Posert from New York to Northern California to oversee both. Advertising executive Rene Henry was hired to run the Los Angeles office. Both Posert and Henry had little to no experience with wine. "I stopped in Memphis on my way to California," said Posert, a Tennessee native. "Some friends of mine gave me a wine tasting. That was my experience. I drank bourbon and still do. But there are so many facts about wine that you could never know them all, so it's okay to say, 'I don't know but I'll get back to you.'"

OFF TO A ROUGH START

"The first group of Edelman staff assigned to work on the account just didn't want to represent California wines. They saw it as below their status," said Posert. "Within a year I had to change several staff people. Monthly reports became the key to success, and I would review those with Harry [Serlis] monthly at the Palace Hotel restaurant in San Francisco."

Posert and his team encountered another big hurdle to obtaining positive coverage of the California wine industry: a dearth of wine reporters.

"In 1965, there were six people who wrote about wine regularly in the United States," said Posert. "We had to create a context whereby wine stories could run in the food, travel, business, feature, science, and other sections, while creating the wine writer community, which now numbers over a thousand."

Edelman needed to change the landscape, so they took the show on the road. "We said, 'the enemies of California wine are ignorance and prejudice,'" said Posert. "So we set up a thousand tastings, hiring 10 people across the country. We let small consumer groups buy European wines under $10, and then we'd buy California wines under $5. The wines would

WINE

THE WEAKLY BOOZ MAGAZINE

TOUTER ON A TOOT...
Blurred Image for an Image-maker

CALIFORNIA

WINES of CALIFORNIA

EDELMAN OF EDELMAN

VOL. 85 NO. 23

Edelman staffers mocked up this *Time*-like cover as an irreverent tribute to Dan's work on behalf of the Wine Institute.

be tasted blind by the groups, who, naturally, 75 percent of the time, preferred the softer, sweeter California wines."

A wide range of magazines and newspapers picked up the story, including *Time, Reader's Digest, House Beautiful, Esquire,* and even *Playboy*. The White House started serving California wines at state dinners. An even bigger break came on the *Tonight Show*, when Edelman arranged for movie star Vincent Price to hold a wine taste test with Johnny Carson. By chance, Zsa Zsa Gabor appeared as a guest and joined the festivities.

"They [Price and Gabor] both got very involved," said Dan. "She said, 'Ah, vine tasting. I vas *veened on vine*.' Everyone said, 'that's great. We'll really get her involved.' Incredible personality, and great for the California Wine Institute to have that exposure."

After landing the P.R. account for the Wine Institute in 1965, Edelman helped California showcase its wines to the world. Here, two women survey a map of the state's wine regions while sampling the product.

The Edelman P.R. program lasted for more than a decade, leading to the famous 1976 Judgment of Paris wine tasting, at which a distinguished panel of European wine experts selected California chardonnays and cabernet sauvignons over their French counterparts. The results, well chronicled in books and the movie *Bottle Shock,* amazed the world. But, as *Wine Spectator* pointed out, the seeds to success had been planted long before. The magazine wrote:

> While the victors in this tasting (and even some of the runners-up) received a tidal wave of publicity, what often seems overlooked, or minimized, is that California already had a burgeoning wine industry – and a lot of excellent wines. And with or without the Paris Tasting, California would have gone on to become exactly what it is – one of the world's premier wine-producing regions. That is more evolution than revolution.

In 1975, United Vintners, California's second largest winemaker after Gallo, pulled out of the Wine Institute, and Governor Jerry Brown ended the one-cent tax on wine that paid for the industry's marketing efforts. Without any funding, the Wine Institute had to end its relationship with Edelman.

"We brought wine to America, and California wine to the world," said Posert.

LONDON CALLING

The Wine Institute account, Edelman's most international up to that time, fueled Dan's desire to stretch his firm overseas. In 1967, he organized a "vacation" to London. Instead of spending his days strolling through Hyde Park, however, Dan got in touch with John Peters, the Gillette representative in England, and asked him to schedule meetings with the top P.R. people in town. Peters reached out to a young, talented executive named Michael Morley.

Though the heir apparent at Harris and Hunter public relations in London, Morley longed for an international public relations outfit, a yen he developed while stationed in Germany as member of the British military. Morley had married a German woman and decided that international communications was the wave of the future

At Harris and Hunter, Morley worked for a variety of consumer and health care clients, including Gillette. Peters was impressed with Morley, less so with the firm. He encouraged Morley to move out on his own, promising him a healthy share of the Gillette business if he did.

Morley chuckled when he received the call from Peters.

Said Morley: "John Peters called me and said, 'I have this P.R. person coming over and he wants me to introduce him to other P.R. people. Well, you're the only other P.R. person I know. Can't you take him off my hands for a little bit? His name is Dan Edelman.'"

Morley, Peters, and Dan met for lunch at an upscale Pall Mall club. Peters stayed for introductions before excusing himself to return to other business. Morley quickly discovered Dan envisioned something more than a meet-and-greet.

"It was clear that he'd built a successful business in the United States, but it had, up to that point, no real international reach. Obviously, he was interested in putting this right, seeing the way public relations was going," said Morley. "So our two agendas meshed beautifully. Dan could expand internationally, and I could get a chance to help create and expand a first-class public relations network."

By the end of the meal, Morley and Dan had hammered out an agreement to open an Edelman office in London, while also looking to the European continent for further opportunities. Morley would quit Harris and Hunter, and rent space on Dover Street. Dan would send operating funds for the new London office as soon as he returned home. He had a bit of parting advice for Morley: make sure to wear longer socks and try to have your teeth fixed.

Morley got his pearly whites worked on, but the funds from America never arrived. In the days

Michael Morley agreed to open Edelman's first international office – in London – after a lunch meeting with Dan in 1967. Morley would stay with the firm until 2006.

of foreign exchange controls, the Edelman office had no idea how to transfer money abroad. Finally they sent a U.S. check, which no one in England could figure out how to cash.

"So I raised the money myself," said Morley. "I just went to a British bank, and said we're doing this thing, there should be some investment forthcoming. But we have a good thing going here. By then I'd started up, and gotten some clients signed up."

Morley shared Dan's bullish outlook on the field of public relations.

"The public relations industry in England was developing just as it was in the United States," said Morley. "We're talking about the Mad Men era. Possibly even madder. It was swinging London.

Short skirts and flowery shirts. The era of the Beatles and the Rolling Stones. It was a lot of fun. And great business as well."

Morley's initial competition would come not from other agencies, but from advertising, the bigger giant. "They were really the enemy. Because they had leverage. They could go international quite easily. They could open an office down the corridor and call it the P.R. department. They could bring in a journalist and start writing press releases to fit the ad strategy."

Dan, Morley, and the young London office knew they'd need a strong selling point to compete for clients with the British advertising firms. They found it in a mantra Dan started preaching the day he opened his first office: the value of independent P.R.

An independent public relations agency could offer clients cost-effective, tailor-made programs in a way advertising agencies or conglomerates could not, Dan argued. Independent P.R. firms didn't have to sell clients on costly packages to appease a parent company or sister agency. Their recommendations would be driven by client needs alone.

"Our major goal is client service, and not service to Wall Street," said Dan. "Our independence allows us to be feisty, hard-hitting, creative, and courageous. And honest. We're the only ones in the position to tell our clients the truth. Public relations is a field of its own. It can only be practiced properly from a standpoint of independence."

The approach caught on in England as it had in the United States. Morley's office grew briskly, bolstered by account work from Gillette and Kimberly-Clark. He hired people like former *Times of London*

"It was swinging London," said Michael Morley about the 1960s when he joined the firm and public relations industry in England was just developing.

journalist David Davis and consumer marketing specialist Audrey Baker.

The agency scored a coup early on when it convinced Princess Anne to tour a new Kimberly-Clark plant in the Northumberland town of Prudhoe, where it manufactured toilet paper and Kotex feminine hygiene pads. All went well until a story appeared in *The Times of London* accusing Davis and Edelman of tricking the princess into visiting the feminine hygiene department on her visit.

"The rest of the press took up the story and it was headlines for a few days until the Buckingham Palace press office put it to rest with a flat denial," said David Davis. "I was told unofficially afterwards that Princess Anne had personally intervened to squelch the story on behalf of Kimberly-Clark and Edelman."

Business came from all quarters, including a mysterious visitor sent by Dan. "I was sitting in the office one day and this guy turns up," said Morley. "He's from Finland. He said, 'We are thinking about extending the Edelman "Finnfacts" operation to Britain and some other countries. You better come to Finland so we can see if we can get along with each other. We have a group of journalists coming over.' So I went, and I quickly realized this meant staying up in the nightclubs with the journalists till god-knows-what hours and drinking yourself silly. Anyway, I passed the test."

Soon after, the Finnfacts Institute told Morley they wanted to expand the Edelman program to Germany. They asked him to use the services of a German man nearing retirement who worked at Infoplan in Hamburg. The firm, part of McCann Erickson, would soon close in a restructuring move. Morley found himself with "a new employee and a new client, and we took over the Infoplan office in Hamburg as well." It was Edelman's first in continental Europe.

ROMANTIC FEVER

In December 1963, when I was 8, I came down with rheumatic fever. The condition, which resulted in a heart murmur, was the result of strep throat run amok. I had to stay in bed for six months to help close a leak in my heart.

Every morning, my mom would come into my cheery room, with its pink walls and red-and-white-striped wallpaper, and open the shades. Then she'd bring me breakfast on a tray. In the evenings, my heart doctor would make a house call (Yes, doctors still made house calls in the 1960s), consulting with my parents at the foot of my bed. My father and I decided that since I had a heart doctor, I didn't have rheumatic fever, I had "romantic fever."

In the afternoons, Richard and John would sit in my bedroom doorway and fill me in on the doings at school. If we laughed too loudly, my mother would warn us to keep quiet so I could rest.

On February 9, 1964, the three of us watched as the Beatles made their first U.S. appearance on *The Ed Sullivan Show*. I declared drummer Ringo Starr my favorite Beatle. My dad set me up with a set of his classical records and a record player. He gave me a notebook so I could log all the music I listened to, by composer. He always said that I became an intellectual in the time of my "romantic fever."

I cherished those tightly organized days, marked by bedside doctor visits, school lessons, after-lunch naps, and after-school visits from Richard and John. Winter turned into spring, and in May 1964 I returned to school. My heart murmur had disappeared, and I had a "normal heart."

Renée Edelman

CHAPTER 6

THE BIG IDEA

When Dan Edelman looked at the top of the public relations industry in the late 1960s, he saw several firms with nearly three times his staff and revenue – Hill & Knowlton, Burson-Marsteller, and Ruder & Finn.

Hill & Knowlton had set up a host of European offices beginning in the 1950s, becoming the go-to firm for large American companies doing business overseas. Burson-Marsteller was in the middle of an international expansion as well, capitalizing on growing industrial P.R. and association work. Ruder & Finn parlayed its extensive Washington, D.C., contacts into large contracts with Bristol-Myers, Gulf & Western, and the governments of Israel and Greece. All offered a full range of services. A "department store" approach, in the words of Harold Burson.

Every agency benefited from a growing trend in corporate America to outsource both advertising and public relations. "By the late 1960s, all the big corporate P.R. departments were gone," said Jack O'Dwyer, longtime industry watcher and publisher of the *O'Dwyer P.R. Newswire.* "The corporations found that all the creativity was in the agency side. Plus the agencies could be honest, they could tell them off. If you're a P.R. executive in a corporation, you can't tell the boss off."

To catch up with the top firms, Edelman needed to do two things: build its presence abroad and prove it could handle large government relations work. Dan

THE 25 LARGEST U.S. PR OPERATIONS

Rankings are based on data submitted to the 1974 O'Dwyer's Directory of Public Relations Firms.

	1973 Net Fee Income[1]	Total Employees
1. Hill and Knowlton	$9,800,000	341
2. Burson-Marsteller*	$7,601,000[2]	320
3. Carl Byoir & Associates	—	248
4. Ruder & Finn	$6,600,000	235
5. J. Walter Thompson PR (including Dialog)*	$6,250,000	305
6. Infoplan International (Interpublic)*	$4,600,000[4]	124
7. Harshe-Rotman & Druck	$3,820,000[4]	143
8. Communications Board[5]	$2,981,000	122
9. Daniel J. Edelman	$2,807,426	136
10. Booke and Co.	$2,713,494	93
11. Ketchum, MacLeod & Grove PR Dept.*	$2,500,000[4]	91
12. Doremus & Co.*	$2,353,000	92
13. PPR International (Young & Rubicam)*	$2,200,000	130
14. Manning, Selvage & Lee	$2,121,909[6]	66
15. The Rowland Co.	$1,834,000[4]	61
16. Georgeson & Co.	$1,750,000	35
17. Rogers, Cowan & Brenner	$1,700,000	67
18. Edward Gottlieb & Assocs.	$1,200,000	46
19. Coordinated Communications*	$1,200,000	39
20. N.W. Ayer & Son*	$1,050,000	42
21. Bell & Stanton	$1,026,042	34
22. Albert Frank-Guenther Law*	$1,000,000	38
23. Underwood, Jordan Assocs.	$900,400	30
24. Dudley-Anderson Yutzy	$896,344	48
25. Hank Meyer Assocs.	$857,055	22

*Ad agency PR Dept. or partner
[1]Net fee income is for 12 months ended June 30, 1973, unless otherwise indicated
[2]Year ended Sept. 30, 1973
[3]Does not include 40 persons abroad in offices partially owned by R&F
[4]Year ended Dec. 31, 1973
[5]Includes Financial Relations Board and Pub Relations Board
[6]MS&L and related companies for years endi Dec. 31, 1972

Copyright 1974 by the J. R. O'Dwyer Co., Inc., 271 Madison Ave., N.Y., N.Y. 10016

> Dan's firm became one the top 10 U.S. P.R. firms, but it struggled to break into the top three.

A Dominant Dozen

The economics and operating methods of the big p.r. firms vary considerably, which is why Hill & Knowlton, with the largest revenues (about $6 million this year), is second to Ruder & Finn on the list below, where the major p.r. firms are ranked according to staff size. H. & K. charges a minimum of $4,000 monthly for its regular corporate clients, which may take their service in several different ways—e.g., by consulting with Chairman Bert Goss for a few days or by having sizable research jobs done by less expensive staff people. Carl Byoir charges a flat $50,000 a year to corporate clients that gross over $30 million. It has twenty-nine such domestic clients, including R.C.A. and Howard Hughes. Total fee income is about $1,600,000; however, the figure does not include staff time charges, which are billed separately. Unlike H. & K., Byoir will not take any client for less than a year. (H. & K. had Svetlana Alliluyeva for just thirteen days, and got $14,600 for its efforts.)

Ruder & Finn, the fastest-growing firm, has a billing system roughly comparable to H. & K.'s and revenues of $4,500,000 a year. R. & F. seems to be the most self-conscious of the firms about p.r. as a business and way of life. Bill Ruder, former Assistant Secretary of Commerce, and David Finn have held or participated in any number of seminars about the proper role for p.r. The firm's client list nowadays includes Bristol-Myers, Gulf & Western, and the Greek and Israeli governments.

Harshe-Rotman & Druck has built full-scale and almost equally large p.r. operations in New York and Chicago, and is rapidly bringing the Los Angeles office up to the same level. Daniel J. Edelman, a Chicago-based firm, emphasizes product promotion. Dudley-Anderson-Yutzy is best known for food-product publicity. Selvage & Lee achieved a postwar reputation for specializing in proxy fights (the most famous was the 1954 fight at Montgomery Ward). The fast-growing Gottlieb, Manning, and Moynahan firms—all formed since World War II—offer the standard line of p.r. services.

T. J. Ross and Earl Newsom are two firms that concentrate almost completely on counseling about corporate policy, and have little or nothing to do with day-to-day press relations. Newsom is interested only in commercial clients that can pay $100,000 for the firm's advice. Ross is the successor firm to the one founded by the late Ivy Lee, and the firm has inherited some of the glamour associated with the man usually considered the father of the business (which is said to have begun when Lee magically transformed John D. Rockefeller from an oil monopolist into a kindly old gentleman who gave dimes to children).

Not listed below are any of the p.r. operations tied to advertising agencies. Interpublic owns Infoplan, which offers a general line of p.r. services, and Thomas J. Deegan Co., basically a counseling firm. Burson-Marsteller is the product of a merger between an ad agency and a p.r. firm. J. Walter Thompson and Young & Rubicam also have sizable p.r. staffs.

	Staff	Clients	Offices
Ruder & Finn	265	105	12
Hill & Knowlton	260	68	16
Carl Byoir	250	35	7
Harshe-Rotman & Druck	150	65	3
Daniel J. Edelman	99	52	5
Dudley-Anderson-Yutzy	92	29	3
Selvage & Lee	75	28	5
Edward Gottlieb	65	23	5
Farley Manning	49	17	3
John Moynahan	45	24	2
T. J. Ross	26	25	2
Earl Newsom	25	12	1

instructed Michael Morley to continue to build a network of affiliates throughout Europe, while looking for potential acquisitions or professionals who could open new Edelman offices.

The firm then tackled its largest public affairs account to-date.

DIRECTING THE MAIL

Direct mail in the United States dates back to the beginning of the U.S. Postal Service. Aaron Montgomery Ward sent out his first catalog in 1872, while Richard Sears mailed his *Book of Bargains: A Money Saver for Everyone* two decades later. In the late 1960s, Lester Wunderman, the "father of direct marketing," expanded the practice to include 1-800 numbers, loyalty programs, and magazine subscription cards.

As direct mail grew, so too did opposition. Adversaries spread falsehoods about the industry, including claims that direct mail was subsidized by first-class mail and that it threatened the Postal Service. The most vocal "junk mail" opponents enlisted the support of media and legislators in attempts to ban the growing business.

Direct mail companies, splintered across all industries, had never acted as a whole to counter the untruths. With opposition heating up, they needed to act. The Direct Mail Marketing Association asked Edelman to help.

The firm immediately targeted four influential groups for education about the benefits of the $50 million trade – the media, legislators and government officials, consumer advocates, and DMMA members. Edelman organized press conferences and media interviews for direct mail leaders, created collateral materials and television and radio clips, and enlisted Bess Myerson, the first Jewish Miss America, as a spokeswoman.

But Edelman didn't simply want to counter misperceptions about the industry. It wanted to turn the negative allegations into an asset. In 1971, after a series of meetings with DMMA leadership, the team came up with a plan – the Mail Preference Service, which allowed Americans to opt out of mailing lists. If people didn't want to receive direct mail, all they had to do was say no.

Direct mail critics had suddenly lost their best argument. Legislators dropped their bills. Most consumer advocates and government officials applauded the move, strengthened their relationship with the DMMA, and would go on to work with them on future issues, including industry-led privacy protections and an anti-pornography effort called "Keep the Mail Clean."

Rather than simply serving as a client's mouthpiece, Edelman established a reputation for examining current practices and identifying where clients and advocates could work together. This direct, no-holds-barred approach, a reflection of Dan's personality, appealed to clients that valued straightforward counsel.

BOWLING FOR PRESIDENTS

As the firm helped defuse the direct mail controversy, Dan saw that he needed a stronger office in Washington, D.C., where he had established a presence after winning the Wine Institute account in 1967. He turned to John Meek, a straight-talking Oklahoman who had penned President John F. Kennedy's "Man on the Moon" speech and served in several high-level positions in the administration of Lyndon Johnson.

Dan had hired Meek for the Edelman Chicago office, but after Meek began to bring in new business based in the nation's capital, including the National Cable Television Association account, Dan placed him in charge of the Edelman D.C. office. Overnight it became a credible public relations force in town, one that would help several clients face a series of government-related challenges.

But first they'd have a little fun.

Through Edelman's work on behalf of bowling equipment maker Brunswick, the D.C. office landed an account to promote bowling on behalf of the National Bowling Council, a collection of manufacturers, bowling center owners, and the professional bowling leagues. The sport had slipped in popularity and repute in recent years.

President Nixon bowling in the Old Executive Office Building in 1971. With help from the National Bowling Council, Edelman arranged for this bowling alley to be built.

When brainstorming ways to grab the public's attention, Meek had an idea. President Richard Nixon enjoyed the sport. Why not organize a media event with the president bowling a few frames? Better yet, why not build a bowling lane for the president? The White House loved the idea.

After months of planning and construction, Meek gathered the top Bowling Council representatives and took them to the White House to meet the president, who had an aide present them with presidential cufflinks and pins. The group then walked over to the Old Executive Office Building to inspect the president's new bowling lane. The large White House press corps jockeyed to record the event.

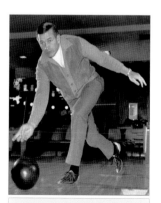

Johnny Unitas, famed quarterback of the Baltimore Colts, rolls a ball in a photo arranged by Meek and his team to promote the sport.

"The next day the photo of Nixon bowling was on the front page of every newspaper in America and the entire front page of the *New York Daily News*," said Meek.

The good press rolled on.

"We arranged for a photo with Johnny Unitas of the Baltimore Colts bowling a few days before he played in a Super Bowl and that photo was used in various media for years afterward," said Meek. "I also got a special bowling stamp, only the fourth sport so honored at that time by the Postal Service."

COINING A NEW SPECIALTY

In 1970, Edelman began work on a little-known account that would pay big dividends for client and agency alike.

As a fund-raising effort, the World Wildlife Fund partnered with Spink, a London-based international coin company, to produce a series of 24 gold and silver coin collections to be sold in 24 participating countries around the world. Part of the proceeds went to the preservation of wildlife. Edelman was hired to build support for the coins among government and business leaders in each country.

In Europe, the London office arranged for Prince Bernhard of the Netherlands, then the WWF's international president, to flip one of the coins at a World Cup soccer match in Germany. Not to be outdone, the Edelman Washington, D.C., office convinced officials at the National Football League to use the WWF coins for all their coin tosses that season.

At the end of the global effort, Spink said the public relations campaign helped sell more coin sets than all the advertising efforts combined. The payoff for Edelman would continue for decades. The work allowed Michael Morley to expand the firm's international network and demonstrated that the agency could handle a global account. It also set the stage for the firm's pioneering work in environmental public relations in the years to come.

BUCKLING UP

The success of the WWF and Bowling Council campaigns made Dan feel good about his decision to place a well-connected man like Meek in charge of the D.C. office. The firm would rely heavily on Meek's relationships in 1971, when the U.S. Department of Transportation proposed a controversial regulation to replace seat belts with air bags in new cars beginning in 1974.

Seat belts saved thousands of lives. The problem was that a majority of Americans refused to use them. To solve this, Ralph Nader and several consumer groups advocated their elimination in favor of the automatic air bags. For their part, auto manufacturers pointed to several drawbacks of the early air bags, including potentially harmful impacts on children and loud explosions that damaged eardrums and startled drivers trying to steer their way through accidents. Neither side argued for both seat belts and air bags.

After the U.S. Department of Transportation proposed a controversial regulation to replace seat belts with air bags, Edelman and the American Seat Belt Council pushed for mandatory seat belt laws to reduce fatalities.

At first, the seat belt manufacturers, not wanting to look self-serving, questioned whether or not they should fight the proposed regulation. Meek implored them to do so, asserting that lives and livelihoods were on the line. "My response was something like this," he said. "We finally have seat belts in our vehicles. They were put there through a DOT rule over the objections of the vehicle manufacturers. This is your business and the federal government has no right to put you out of the business of making a product that is proven to save lives. And you ought to fight it."

Fight it they did. Working in typical D.C. fashion, Edelman and the American Seat Belt Council reached out to anyone who could help save the belts from elimination. They approached the Senate Commerce Committee to get the regulation modified to keep seat belts in cars along with air bags. Edelman and the council pushed for mandatory seat belt use laws similar to ones in Australia that had cut fatalities dramatically. They also fought for seat belts through the media, though were careful never to pair industry leaders in on-air debates with the wily Nader.

After years of contentious discussion, the Department of Transportation delayed its air bag regulations until the technology advanced. When they did mandate air bags, they were to supplement seat belts, not replace them. By the mid-1970s, several automakers offered both air bags and three-point shoulder seat belts in new cars, which would later become the industry norm.

"There wouldn't be a seat belt industry without Edelman," said American Seat Belt Council President Charles Pulley.

"Our team lobbied for the seat belt manufacturers, and every time I read of a life saved because of seat belts I'm proud of what we did," said Meek.

GETTING CREATIVE

By 1975, Edelman counted more than 100 companies and organizations on its client roster. It employed 150 people and billed more than $3 million annually, making it one of the country's top 10 P.R. firms. Dan changed the name of the firm to Daniel J. Edelman, Inc., to reflect the maturation. He moved the Chicago headquarters from the Merchandise Mart to larger offices at 221 North LaSalle Street.

Investor relations – including annual reports, company newsletters, and shareholder communications – accounted for a quarter of all Edelman business, while its government relations work made up a growing 15 percent. Despite its diversification, the agency was still known for its strength in consumer marketing public relations.

Some consumer campaigns struck a chord – school art competitions for Gillette's Paper Mate

Pens, corn-eating contests with Kraft Squeeze Parkay, and footwear fashion shows with George Hamilton for the Sole Leather Council. Other efforts bombed, including a "Sweet Success" slimming trial featuring Mars candy bars.

Actor-producer George Hamilton, known for his sartorial style, was a spokesperson for the Sole Leather Council, one of Edelman's successful consumer accounts in the 1970s.

Dan encouraged his employees to keep trying, constantly pushing them to come up with the "Big Idea." He once recounted an experience from his days at Columbia. During an important test, Dan filled three notebooks to answer a question. A classmate wrote a single paragraph and received an A. After that, Dan realized smart work was just as important as hard work.

In a speech to his staff early in the decade, Dan said creativity was "too often ignored by public relations people" even though it marked "the difference between good and mediocre programs." He advocated a thorough and open approach to creativity, one that involved extensive research and brainstorming sessions. The most creative employees, he counseled, were the ones who "continue to be current" and who take their role as a "listening post" seriously.

"Reach for the Big Ideas that will make it work," said Dan. "Package it, stage it, dramatize it. Create excitement. Sure, they'll be some flak from time

After being crowned Miss America in 1971, Phyllis George traveled the U.S. for Toni and the pageant's other sponsors.

to time; you'll get some kidding. But I suggest that over a long period of time the result will be much greater than merely sending it along as a regular news release."

For Toni, the "Big Idea" had been conceived back in 1958 when Dan convinced the company to become a primary sponsor of the annual Miss America contest. Toni and other Gillette products would be used by contestants during the pageant, and then Edelman would help organize promotional appearances around the country featuring the new Miss America.

In 1971, approximately 80 million television viewers watched Texan Phyllis George claim the crown. She sported Toni products, attended the Toni-sponsored reception following the event, and then toured 200,000 miles around the nation representing Toni and the other sponsors.

THE WORLD'S MOST FINICKY CAT

With the Toni Twins, years before, Dan had taken a popular advertising campaign and turned it into a real-life phenomenon, ushering in the era of modern marketing public relations. History repeated itself in the 1970s, when a series of consumer companies asked his firm to do the same.

Leo Burnett Advertising had struck gold in 1968

when it created Morris the Cat as the "spokescat" for 9Lives cat food. The orange tabby and "World's Most Finicky Cat," a rescue from the Hinsdale, Illinois, Humane Society, enthralled viewers with his dry voice-over put-downs of competing cat foods, quickly becoming one of the most beloved and popular stars in America.

Wanting to broaden the Morris brand, 9Lives reached out to Edelman for ideas. It wanted activities to make Morris more of an actual, relatable feline, while strengthening the tie between Morris and the 9Lives label. The Edelman consumer team, led by Judith Rich in Chicago, came up with an idea: If the public couldn't get enough of Morris, why not give them more Morrises?

Morris the Cat.

They launched a 9-City, 9Lives Morris Look-Alike contest. Morris traveled to each city to help with the judging, appearing with his feline resemblances on countless hours of television shows. The success prompted 9Lives and Edelman to expand the competition nationwide.

The following year, Edelman had another proposition. If 9Lives wanted Morris to come across as nonfictional, he should do what human stars often do when they reach a high level of fame – pen a biography. Along with writer Mary Daniels of the *Chicago Tribune* and William Morrow Publishing, 9Lives produced *Morris, An Intimate*

Biography. The book climbed the bestseller lists. Morris and his team penned several other books, with the cat going on book tours to support each one. When he traveled, Morris and his handler flew first class, while Edelman and 9Lives staffers sat in coach.

Poster for the Morris Look-Alike contest.

Throughout the decade, Edelman took Morris to numerous segments of society. The firm developed "The Morris," a bronze statuette given to local cat clubs as an award for the "best household pet." Working in conjunction with the American Humane Society, Edelman initiated Adopt-A-Cat Month, which led to the adoption of a million strays, a fitting response, since Morris himself had been one.

When Morris died in 1978, some of his handlers pressed to substitute a look-alike in secret. Edelman and 9Lives adopted the opposite approach, letting the media know that the original Morris had passed away and allowing his fans to grieve for him. "Morris, the Cat, 17, Dead," read the headline in *The New York Times*. After an appropriate period of mourning, Edelman helped introduce a new Morris.

Morris, An Intimate Biography made bestseller lists and was the first of several books to chronicle the travels of the 9Lives icon.

Morris continued to bask in the media and public spotlight when Edelman helped him run for president in 1988 and again in 1992, campaigns devised by creative genius Pam Talbot, who'd worked on the account since joining the

Morris the Cat kicked off his candidacy for president in 1987 at the National Press Club. The campaign idea was the brainchild of Edelman's Pam Talbot. Eleanor Mondale (far right), daughter of former Vice President Walter Mondale, was Morris's campaign manager.

Chicago office as an account executive in 1972. Eleanor Mondale, daughter of former Vice President Walter Mondale, kicked off the Morris candidacy in 1987 at the National Press Club in Washington, D.C. "Kennedy cleared the way for Catholics, Ferraro for women, and Morris will overcome the hurdle that to date has excluded animals," said Mondale. The Edelman account team couldn't resist the groaners, having Morris declare such "pawlicies" as "Walk softly and carry a big can opener" and "Things were simpler when Iran belonged to the Persians." According to opinion polls, Morris had higher name recognition than Bob Dole, Michael Dukakis, and the rest of the presidential field.

FINGER LICKIN'

Work for one of Edelman's longest and most wide-ranging accounts began in 1975, when the firm helped another advertising icon, Colonel Sanders and Kentucky Fried Chicken, to find countless public relations opportunities. Like most of the firm's long-term consumer accounts, this one started with a focus on product publicity – and the star himself.

With his white suit, black string tie, and silver mustache and goatee, Harland David "Colonel"

Harland David "Colonel" Sanders, with his iconic white suit, black string tie, and silver mustache and goatee.

impromptu stop at a Greenwich Village Kentucky Fried Chicken outlet, where Sanders berated the owner for mashed potatoes that tasted like "wallpaper paste," brown gravy "sludge," and "the worst fried chicken I've ever seen." "For the Colonel, It Was Finger-Lickin' Bad," ran the headline the next day.

The colonel died in 1980, but the company and Edelman continued to promote his image, dropping a skydiving Colonel Sanders over Sandwich, Illinois, to promote a new chicken sandwich offering and arranging for hundreds of colonel clones to stage massive chicken dances in Times Square and Beijing. The colonel even played a central role when Edelman helped the company rebrand itself from Kentucky Fried Chicken to KFC.

For more than a quarter century, the KFC account evolved and branched into many areas, including community relations, multicultural outreach, corporate communications, and health and nutrition, often setting industry firsts. Edelman helped KFC develop public relations programs with DARE (Drug Abuse Resistance Education), the YWCA, and senior citizen organizations promoting entrepreneurship.

To Dan, the KFC account would become one of his favorites, not only for the size and length of the work, but the willingness of KFC leaders to embrace his firm's counsel. He watched as his firm's areas of expertise grew right along with the account.

Dan felt he and his firm gave everything they had to KFC. But by the end of the account, Dan did not view the relationship as being reciprocal. In a speech to KFC franchisees, he stood up for public relations and for his agency and delivered a blunt message: "If I may say so, you're behind the times in putting all of your dollars into advertising. Even doubling the public relations budget would still represent just 1 percent of your total marketing expenditures. There's also the problem

Sanders knew the power of public relations from the day he opened his first store in Corbin, Kentucky. Though he sold the corporation in 1964, Sanders had remained active in promoting its products. Edelman arranged hundreds of appearances for him around the U.S. to promote new menu items. Staffers soon learned his participation could be a double-edged sword.

After a lunch in Manhattan that Edelman arranged for the colonel with *New York Times* restaurant critic Mimi Sheraton, the duo made an that more work is assigned and budgets are cut during the year. For this year to date, we have spent 145 percent of the fee on people time, leading to a steep loss.

"In addition to budget, we need respect. It's essential we have an opportunity to meet with senior executives of your company in addition to your public relations director. We've experienced too much turnover in personnel based on orders from KFC."

KFC and Edelman parted ways shortly thereafter. The loss of the account crushed Dan.

"A FUNNY LOOKING FARMER WITH A FUNNY SOUNDING NAME"

Edelman didn't have to compete with advertising on another major account. Hunt-Wesson Foods planned to introduce a first-of-its-kind line of "gourmet" popping corn without advertising, relying instead on Edelman and the efforts of the brand's creator, Orville Clarence Redenbacher, a self-professed "funny looking farmer with a funny sounding name."

Redenbacher had perfected his superior-tasting popcorn by testing thousands of corn hybrids on a farm outside Valparaiso, Indiana. In 1976, Redenbacher sold the company to Hunt-Wesson Foods. Like Sanders, Redenbacher agreed to continue to promote the brand, always appearing in his trademark horn-rimmed glasses and bow tie. His corn was twice as fluffy as any other brand, but many stores refused to stock it because it was also twice as expensive.

Edelman's first efforts involved getting the product onto store shelves. To do this, they arranged for Orville Poppin' Press Parties in major markets, taking Redenbacher on the road to show media and VIPs that his corn was worth every penny. They were hooked, both on the popcorn and Orville's folksy charm. Hunt-Wesson was thrilled.

Orville Clarence Redenbacher in his trademark horn-rimmed glasses and bow tie, showing off his first-of-its-kind line of gourmet popping corn. Redenbacher would visit the Edelmans at home and teach Richard, Renée, and John how to make popcorn.

". . . after Orville's personal appearance interviews on television, radio and newspapers, the consumer interest and heavy sales from the stores which did stock the product soon convinced the other accounts to climb on the bandwagon," wrote the company. "Further evidence in the direct correlation between the effect of the publicity and the strength of our business is indicated by the fact that where we had the

A seven-story hot air balloon in the shape of a popped kernel of corn flew over festivals to draw attention to Redenbacher's popcorn, which became the nation's dominant brand.

Ruth and Dan were fixtures on the Chicago social scene. Here they are pictured with Mayor Richard Daley and his wife, Eleanor.

"At the same time, Edelman was discovering the potential for a different and more potent kind of P.R. with the consumer a critical element of the storytelling and with true stories holding the power to move opinion more forcefully than manufactured spots. In fact, these efforts, with their origins clearly linked to the Toni Twins campaigns, helped lead the way to the rising authority of public relations."

HOME SUPPORT

"Orville Redenbacher came over for dinner and taught us how to make popcorn," said Richard Edelman. "Phyllis George came over, too. She was Miss America and, man, that was big bragging rights for a kid."

greatest number of interviews and newspaper stories, our sales have been strongest."

Hunt-Wesson urged Edelman to keep the momentum going with more appearances and activities for Redenbacher. Edelman concocted nationwide "Pop Art" contests, with entries made entirely from the corn, and launched a seven-story hot air balloon in the shape of a popped kernel of corn to fly at festivals. The media and public continued their love affair with Redenbacher, who became a cultural icon of the era, while the popcorn he created became the nation's dominant brand.

"The 9Lives, KFC, and Orville Redenbacher campaigns were created at a time when advertising led – always and powerfully," said Pam Talbot. "Public relations, though, could walk characters off the small screen and into the real world, lifting Morris, Orville, and Colonel Sanders from product symbols to resonant, relatable beings. That metamorphosis added staying power and helped the brands gain a relationship with consumers that wouldn't have been possible with advertising alone."

With the Edelmans, home and firm often overlapped. Ruth's parties continued to grow, with 300 business leaders and journalists gathering regularly in the Edelman apartment on North Astor Street. When they weren't hosting at home, Ruth and Dan attended social functions around town with groups like the Young Presidents Organization, mixing a good time with an undercurrent of business.

Though she didn't have an office at Edelman, Ruth helped expand the business as much as anyone at the firm. With Dan often out of town, she also ran the home and oversaw the children's education. Her standards for excellence were as exacting as Dan's.

"My mother was determined that we were going to succeed. She was the superintendent of the kids," said Richard. "We had tutors from a very early age. I had a speech coach. I had a weightlifting coach, because I was too scrawny. I remember being 16 and she would get me up in [Charlevoix] Michi-

Ruth and Dan chat with Sargent Shriver at the opening of an exhibition at the Chicago Art Institute.

gan to do my circuit training for football. With a stopwatch. Coach Ruth. And she organized neighborhood kids into doing math and English lesson plans produced by a company called Science Research Associates. From age 7 or 8 we'd be in Charlevoix working on these damn things with the neighborhood kids. It was like study hall."

The results paid off.

"It's something that we looked forward to, that our children would live a better life if they got better grades," said Ruth. "And they did. They got all A's and B's."

When Ruth grew disillusioned with the local school, she hatched a plan.

"Dick Day, the headmaster of Exeter, was speaking at YPO," Ruth said. "I was sitting in the front row with my legs crossed, trying to get his attention so I could talk with him after his speech. And I did. I told him about Richard. He said, 'Come on up and stay with us.' So we did. Richard enrolled right away."

All three children, in fact, would attend Exeter, a prestigious private boarding school in New Hampshire, then go on to Ivy League universities – Richard to Harvard, Renée to Yale, and John to Brown. Ruth hung their diplomas in Dan's study.

DAN'S SMARTEST BUSINESS DECISION

When I was young, I saw my parents' marriage as a modern-day *Pygmalion*, the 1912 George Bernard Shaw play that was later made into the Broadway musical and Hollywood movie *My Fair Lady*, the latter starring Rex Harrison and Audrey Hepburn. To this day, that movie remains my parents' favorite.

In my young eyes, my mother was Eliza Doolittle – energetic, shy, and eager to better herself. My father, nine years her senior, was her Henry Higgins. Ruth's hardscrabble upbringing in Racine, Wisconsin, stood in contrast to Dan's more privileged and sophisticated youth in New York City.

As I reached my teenage years and went away to school, I began to see my parents' relationship more realistically and questioned the roles in which I had cast them. Had Dan really taught Ruth "everything she knows," as Higgins claimed he had in turning Eliza into a lady?

Ruth and Dan complemented each other. "We're a team," is how my mother describes their union. She is the warm people-person who can charm a CEO within minutes. At the dinner table, my parents often talked about business, my father always valuing my mother's counsel and creative ideas. When I would see them together, whether out on the town or entertaining at home, I would often think that Ruth was the smartest business decision my father ever made.

At my father's 90th birthday party, held at the Casino Club in Chicago, Ruth, resplendent in a long blue evening gown, her hair done up in a French twist, and Dan, dapper in a dark suit and red Hermès tie, blew out the birthday candles together. Then they danced cheek-to-cheek to "Tenderly" by Johnny Mathis, their favorite love song.

Renée Edelman

CHAPTER 7

BRANCHING OUT

By the mid-1970s, Dan had assembled a team of highly talented public affairs and issue-management specialists in his offices, including Dick Aurelio in New York, John Meek in Washington, D.C., and Michael Morley and David Davis in London. Edelman would need them all to pull off its largest international challenge to date, a deeply controversial issue that stretched across the Atlantic to the shores of both Europe and the U.S.

In 1962, the British and French governments had signed a formal treaty to develop a supersonic passenger jet that would travel at twice the speed of sound, cutting normal flight times in half. Named Concorde – after the English and French words for "unity" – the new jets were a risky business proposition from the outset. Design issues, cost overruns, and the 1973 oil crisis had forced many international airlines to cancel their orders even before the first plane rolled off the production line.

Spurred to action by environmentalists and citizens groups concerned about sonic booms, the U.S. Congress banned Concorde flights from landing in the United States, dealing a crippling blow to the fledgling enterprise. If Concorde were to have any chance of surviving, its primary carriers, Air France and British Air, would need to provide service to the lucrative U.S. market.

The Concorde in flight at the Farnborough International Airshow in Hampshire, England.

The pro- and anti-Concorde camps rallied, spending millions on lawyers, lobbyists, and public relations people. Edelman led the P.R. efforts in support of the Concorde, with Meek, Aurelio, and Morley spearheading Edelman programs in their respective localities.

The team quickly realized that opposition ran highest in New York, so they decided to first focus on lifting the ban in Washington, D.C., where Dulles Airport was under the control of the Department of Transportation. After debunking several myths perpetrated by opponents and stirring excitement for the supersonic jets in the nation's capital, Edelman helped convince Department of Transportation Secretary William Coleman to allow the planes to land at Dulles on an 18-month trial basis.

"None of the scary scenarios came to pass," said Michael Morley. "All it did, which was what we had been planning for all along, was to make New York envious because it didn't have the flight."

Turning its efforts to New York, Edelman helped ease noise concerns by organizing community meetings, where Concorde proponents played audiotapes comparing the sound of Concorde takeoffs to those of 747 and 727 jet airliners. The differences were negligible. At the same time, Edelman organized support from members of the New York business community, who wanted to be able to travel back and forth between John F. Kennedy Airport and London or Paris in half the current time.

Newly elected President Jimmy Carter was forced to get into the discussions about the flights during his first few months in office. "During his campaign for the U.S. presidency, Jimmy Carter had opposed the Concorde," said Meek. "But one day the White House called and asked me to choose somebody to come to meet with the president to make our case. I chose a veteran congressman from New York. The rest is history."

Carter lifted the ban nationally in February 1977, but the Port Authority of New York and New Jersey, which oversees JFK Airport operations, refused to lift its own local ban, prompting Edelman to stage yet more community meetings and promote new studies that continued to demonstrate that Concorde flights would be no different from those of other jets. In October 1977, the United States Court of Appeals in Manhattan overturned the local ban, paving the way for Concorde flights at JFK Airport by the end of the year.

In the years to come, Edelman would continue to fight on behalf of the supersonic jets, helping to defeat at least six more attempted bans and many legal challenges. The agency had proved it could handle a global public affairs operation and emerge victorious. Dan and his team savored the results and looked for more such challenges.

The Concorde would fly for 27 years before ending service in 2003, the victim of a global recession and a business model that had never really totally jibed with demand.

WORKING FOR PEANUTS

A year after the Concorde campaign, the U.N. approached Michael Morley and the London office to see if Edelman could help Gambia, Mali, Senegal, Niger, Nigeria, and Sudan market peanut oil to European countries. Peanuts were an important export product for the six poor African nations, and the U.N. wished to give each country's economy a boost.

Morley and a few Edelman staffers set out on an investigatory journey to Africa. After a six-hour ride through the desert to a small village in Senegal – whose survival depended almost entirely on peanut farming – Morley knew that this campaign would be different. "We were met by the entire village," he said. "An elder rose up and gave

Edelman London was hired by the U.N. on behalf of six West African nations whose economic mainstay was peanut farming. The firm's campaign helped spur peanut oil sales in Germany, France, the UK, and Italy.

a most moving speech, saying that if Edelman's work succeeded we would save the lives of the babies in the village."

The Edelman team left Africa highly motivated. The firm quickly rolled out public relations campaigns in Germany, France, the UK, and Italy, where it encouraged food producers to purchase more African peanut oil and reached consumers through newsletters and traditional media. In France, the team built its campaign around a commonly held belief that peanut oil made the best French fries.

Edelman was able to spur African peanut oil sales in Europe for several years and, in the process, help pioneer a new marketing approach that encouraged consumers to consider the welfare of less affluent countries when making purchasing decisions.

A DEAL WITH RICHARD

"It was 1978," said Richard. "I was just three months away from graduating from Harvard Business School when my father pulled me aside and said he'd just been approached by Doyle Dane Bernbach advertising and that they wanted to buy the firm. He said, 'I'll make you a deal. Come work for the firm for one year. If you don't like it, you can leave. But as long as you're here, I'll never sell the business.'"

Dan had received several inquiries from advertising firms about selling his agency since opening Edelman in 1952. Each time he had been tempted, and each time he refused. He believed strongly in the importance of independent public relations. But he also dreamed of someday handing the business over to his children if they were willing and able to take over the firm.

Richard rebuffed his father's offer at first. He had already accepted a junior-level marketing position at Playtex and booked a six-week European vacation with a girlfriend. But Dan persisted and Richard agreed to the deal, but said he'd start after he'd taken his trip to Europe.

"Then, a week before graduation, he called me again," recounted Richard. "He said, 'We just won this account called ContiCommodity Services. You know about commodity futures, and we don't have anybody here who can do that. We need you to start right away.'

"I was desperate for a break after killing myself for two years at school. I told him about my vacation plans. He said, 'I'll give you a vacation in December.'"

Richard finished his exams on a Friday and started work at Edelman the following Monday. He lost the European vacation – and the girlfriend. Dan set him up in the Chicago office as a junior-level account executive with a $25,000 salary. "I learned my first lesson about family business if you're taking it seriously," said Richard. "Leisure is not an option."

Dan wanted Richard to learn the business from the ground up and understand the importance of client relationships. So the newly minted Harvard graduate found himself playing donkey baseball, betting on flying chicken races, and eating Rocky Mountain oysters (bull calf testicles) with Conti-Commodity cotton futures traders at the Lubbock Cotton Conference he helped organize.

Back in Chicago, he wrote press releases and pitched reporters on stories. "I remember George Lazarus from the *Chicago Tribune* calling me up and saying, 'I don't give a damn if you're Dan Edelman's son. This story is crap,'" said Richard.

His bigger struggle surrounded his relationship with Dan. "The truth is," said Richard, "I hadn't been all that close to my father until I started working for him."

From Day 1 their styles clashed. Dan had built the business by hiring people with backgrounds similar to his own – former journalists and marketing public relations experts. Richard joined the company with an MBA approach. Something had to give.

After six months, Richard transferred to the Edelman New York office and the mentorship of general manager Dick Aurelio, a former *Newsday* editor and deputy mayor in the administration of New York City Mayor John Lindsay. "I wouldn't have lasted had I stayed in Chicago," said Richard.

Dick Aurelio, general manager of the New York office in the 1970s, proved a valuable mentor to the young Richard Edelman.

Richard's education in public relations flourished under Aurelio, a seasoned veteran with excellent New York contacts. "He ripped apart my copy," said Richard, "but he also showed me the value of networking with opinion leaders and took me along as he worked on important projects such as the boycott of Nestlé infant formula," which had been organized by people who opposed selling milk substitutes to parents and infants in the developing world.

After several months, Aurelio sent Richard on a field trip with the office's toughest client – Hooker Chemical and Plastics Corporation, the company responsible for dumping toxic waste in the Love Canal neighborhood of Niagara Falls, New York.

"Dick said I should go up and accompany the client to see how bad the situation really was," said Richard. "The client and I actually walked on the Love Canal site. He said to me, 'It really doesn't smell so bad here.' In fact, the smell was so horrible I felt like gagging. I called my mother afterward and she said, 'I hope you were wearing your galoshes. I don't want to have neon green grandchildren.'"

Under the eye of Aurelio, Richard mastered the basics of the public relations business, learning how to network, pitch accounts, and pen compelling copy. In 1981, for his work on behalf of ContiCommodity, which included crisis communications when Conti was accused of manipulating the world silver market along with brothers Nelson Bunker Hunt and William Herbert Hunt of Texas, he won a Silver Anvil, the Public Relations Society of America's top award.

THE CHANGING FACE OF P.R.

From their vantage points in Chicago and New York, respectively, Dan and Richard could both see the outlines of a changing company and an evolving industry.

In 1978, advertising giant Foote Cone & Belding purchased the veteran P.R. firm Carl Byoir

& Associates, launching a buying spree of P.R. firms by ad agencies. Young & Rubicam bought Burson-Marsteller the following year, while J. Walter Thompson purchased Hill & Knowlton in 1980. Within a few years, nearly all the top public relations agencies were owned by large advertising firms. With Richard having decided to remain at Edelman after a year on the job, Dan stayed true to his word and kept his agency independent.

Meanwhile, the public relations workforce was also undergoing a significant transformation. Women made up 41 percent of the workforce in 1979. By 1983, they would be a majority and a quarter century later women would make up more than 70 percent of the P.R. workforce. When Dan founded Edelman, most employees in the field came from a newspaper background. That began to change in the late 1970s and '80s as universities added more public relations classes to their curriculums and a greater number of non-journalists joined the trade.

These trends, both within Edelman and industry-wide, influenced the type of client firms pursued as well as the campaigns they organized. Over the next several years, the agency faced a series of wide-ranging challenges that expanded the firm's capabilities and reputation, while breaking new ground in the field of public relations.

A FRESH START IN L.A.

Since founding his agency in 1952, Dan had always dreamed of having a strong Los Angeles office that would represent West Coast industries and help clients capitalize on the power of Hollywood. The Wine Institute account had given him the opportunity to hire Rene Henry and open a small

Edelman employees Tom Harrison, Shari Jensen Ayre, Barbara Molotsky, and Dan celebrate Harrison's promotion to general manager of the firm's L.A. office.

office in L.A. in 1967. After a few years, fueled by steady work for the California wine industry as well as Sunkist citrus growers, the staff grew to a dozen and Edelman moved to larger quarters.

Dan urged Henry to round up as much new business as possible, with one exception. Early on, Henry had the opportunity to bring on actor Karl Malden as a client. Dan nixed the idea. He didn't want his firm to become known as a Hollywood publicity agency.

When Henry left to form his own agency in 1970, Dan attempted to replace him with a series of experienced managers culled from other Edelman offices. None of them succeeded to Dan's satisfaction. The Los Angeles operation remained profitable for several years, but when Edelman lost the Sunkist work and the Wine Institute account in 1975, the office struggled to stay in business.

On the verge of closing the office in 1978, Dan turned to a 24-year-old account executive in the Edelman Chicago office named Tom Harrison. "I thought he offered me the job because he was tired of losing all these talented veteran employees," said Harrison. "If I failed, what did Dan care? I was just a kid."

Harrison inherited a handful of employees and two small clients, one of them a company that sold pre-made, wine-based cocktails. "We lost both accounts my first month out there," said Harrison. "I thought I was going to be fired. But when I told Dan he said, 'Good. Now everything we do there is all yours.'"

Shortly thereafter, Harrison obtained a request-for-proposal from Toyota's U.S. headquarters in nearby Torrance, California. The carmaker was searching for an agency with a Los Angeles office and a national presence. Despite having no clients, Harrison responded to the RFP and somehow Edelman got on the short list of finalists. Harrison then decided to accompany Toyota executives as they spent a week visiting the offices of Edelman and other firms in Chicago and Washington, D.C. At the end of the week, Toyota gave the million-dollar account to the young Edelman general manager.

"That Toyota account really made us here in L.A.," said Harrison. "We became the hot agency in town, and within the year we signed up Bridgestone, Mattel, and Yoplait yogurt."

After Bridgestone purchased a Firestone plant in Tennessee, Edelman helped the Japanese tire manufacturer strengthen community ties through a P.R. effort that included outreach to government officials, media relations, local events, as well as employee and union communications.

On behalf of Yoplait, a product which was developed in 1964 by two French dairy farmers named Yola and Coplait, Edelman handled public relations for a 1980 marketing effort called, "Get a little taste of French culture." Edelman hit the road. It dispatched a fleet of tasting vans painted to resemble the facade of a French café, hosted a series of bicycle races in key U.S. cities, and gave reporters rides in a hot air balloon that featured a giant Yoplait logo. The creative P.R. and advertising campaigns soon helped propel Yoplait to the top of the American yogurt market.

A MONUMENTAL CHALLENGE

When the Edelman Washington, D.C., office first started to do a little work for a newly formed nonprofit organization in 1981 – the Vietnam Veterans Memorial Fund – it had no idea the job would eventually involve a national debate. In its proposal to the fund, Edelman pledged to implement a wide range of traditional media techniques to promote the "National Statue" that the group wanted to erect on the National Mall in Washington. These

Edelman's work on behalf of the Vietnam Veterans Memorial Fund turned into a much larger, more complex assignment when Maya Lin's controversial design provoked a contentious nationwide debate.

efforts would include press releases, talk show appearances, press conferences, feature stories, and outreach efforts to Vietnam veterans.

Almost as an aside, the firm pledged: "Should there be criticism of the statue, Edelman will work with your officials in responding through letters-to-the-editor, editorial columns, interviews with key reporters, and appearances on radio and television talk shows." Little did anyone suspect that the controversy would erupt into a full-scale battle, reopening many wounds of the Vietnam War itself.

After a national contest that drew more than 1,400 design proposals, the Vietnam Veterans Memorial Fund selected the entry of Maya Lin, a 21-year-old Chinese-American architecture major at Yale University. Lin's design, which would engrave the names of nearly 60,000 dead or missing veterans on, in Lin's words, "a rift in the earth, a long, polished black stone wall emerging from and receding into the earth," won immediate praise from the architecture community.

But the unconventional design also brought howls of protest from opponents, such as Congressman Henry Hyde ("a political statement of shame and dishonor"), gadfly Ross Perot, and Vietnam veterans associations that worried the semi-underground memorial would not properly reflect the service members' valor and sacrifice.

Edelman had been hired primarily to help raise $6 million for the monument's construction and foster support for the design, but now it found itself in the middle of a public opinion firestorm. The firm's focus was no longer on press releases and media events; it now had to insert itself into the process of trying to find a satisfying solution for its client as well as the public at large.

The agency gathered high-profile backers of the design whose support would help preserve Lin's original proposal. The roster included Hollywood actor Bob Hope, Virginia Senator John Warner, first lady Nancy Reagan, Vietnam veteran and Pittsburgh Steelers running back Rocky Blier, and retired Army Chief of Staff General William Westmoreland. At the same time, the Edelman D.C. office arranged meetings between advocates and opponents to see if a compromise could be forged. Edelman recommended the theme, "They Served with Honor," to shift the focus to the men and women who fought in Vietnam.

After a year of contentious debate and backroom maneuvering, a compromise was finally reached. Lin's design would be kept, but the site would include a traditional-looking bronze statue of three American soldiers who appeared to be gazing at the granite slab to view the names of their fallen comrades.

Edelman's handling of the controversy resulted in more than 5,500 printed stories about the memorial, generating contributions from more than a quarter of a million people, which helped the veteran's organization reach its fund-raising goals.

More important, the open give-and-take that Edelman had nurtured brought many opposing factions and agendas together, leaving the country with a stirring monument that in the end helped heal many of the deep wounds left behind by the war. It also showed that thoughtful public relations could play a constructive role in an overheated controversy.

GENERAL OPPOSITION

During the Vietnam Memorial debate, General William Westmoreland had been on Edelman's side. But only a year later, the firm found itself opposing the general in another fractious debate.

CBS hired Edelman to help it defend itself in the court of public opinion after General William Westmoreland brought a lawsuit against the network.

When General Westmoreland hit CBS News with a $120 million lawsuit for libel following the airing of *The Uncounted Enemy: A Vietnam Deception*, a program that accused him of understating the strength and size of the North Vietnamese forces, the network took an extraordinary step. It reached out to a public relations firm for assistance.

A year earlier, CBS's Dan Rather and the program *60 Minutes* had been sued by a California physician who charged that he had been slandered by the network. The press turned against CBS, questioning its newsgathering tactics. CBS did not want the Westmoreland affair to turn into a similar public relations fiasco.

Edelman had the right person for the job, a dogged, well-connected New York P.R. man named John Scanlon. (Richard had convinced his father to purchase Scanlon's public relations firm in 1982.) The bearded, affable Scanlon knew every reporter covering the lawsuit. He plied them with information (and often cocktails) leading up to the trial, then sat next to them every day during the proceedings. *The New York Times* called him "new scenery on the landscape of legal procedure."

"If the Westmoreland people held a press conference, John had arranged a follow-up press conference in an adjoining meeting room and captured all of the people leaving," said Dan.

"Scanlon was superb in getting us a level playing field," said CBS correspondent Mike Wallace, as quoted by "The Holmes Report," a P.R. industry newsletter. "Westmoreland's attorney was threatening to bring down a major news network. Our press people were unable to blunt these thrusts at the integrity of CBS. Scanlon picked all of this up, talked reasonably to reporters, and got CBS to talk candidly about the whole issue. You could see a palpable change in the media because of what Scanlon did."

As press coverage and public opinion began to tilt in favor of the network, Westmoreland dropped his lawsuit. The two sides agreed to allow the case to be decided in the "court of public opinion" rather than in a court of law. In the end, CBS paid no damages.

When the dust had settled, it was clear that Scanlon and Edelman had pioneered a new specialty: litigation public relations. The agency would go on to represent numerous high-profile litigants, ranging from Fortune 500 corporations to Ivana Trump in her divorce from "The Donald." The tactics it perfected during the CBS-Westmoreland trial would be studied by all the other full-service public relations firms as well as new boutique agencies that were springing up to specialize in litigation P.R.

"I think it's a very natural development of the legal process as it relates to the media," said Dan in a *Chicago Sun-Times* story. "The media demand an avalanche of material, and we know it's important to their jobs and the fair presentation of the case that they get everything they need."

Scanlon took a break from New York P.R. to represent Corazon Aquino in her successful presidential bid against Ferdinand Marcos in the Philippines. Though Edelman did not receive monetary remuneration for the campaign, Aquino's stunning victory gave the agency excellent positive publicity all around the world as well as a P.R. account with the new Philippine government.

Edelman's handling of these well-known public affairs victories broadened the firm's reputation, allowing it to compete with industry leaders like Hill & Knowlton and Burson-Marsteller for larger, international government relations contracts.

TALKING TURKEY

While Edelman's worldwide profile grew, its reputation rested on – and most of its revenues still derived from – its consumer campaigns, which were now led by Pam Talbot in Chicago. Though half his physical size, Talbot was every ounce Dan's match. She was as hardworking, smart, and single-focused as the company's founder.

Talbot was adept at both winning new business and keeping older accounts fresh and current. She led the company's efforts to move campaigns for clients like KFC and Orville Redenbacher into new territory, fusing company creativity with

Every year since 1981, a team of experts has staffed the Butterball Turkey Talk-Line to answer calls from harried holiday cooks suffering from "turkey trauma."

the needs of the client. She also understood Dan Edelman better than anyone at the company, including Richard. Her unique blend of skills paid big dividends for the consumer accounts.

At the same time that Edelman was entering its second decade of service to clients like Kraft Foods and Hunt-Wesson, the firm brought in a new crop of consumer clients, including Butterball. Talbot and her team would propel the turkey-and-meat company to the top of the industry with a first-of-its-kind P.R. campaign.

During a 1981 brainstorming session on how to promote a product as common as turkey, Talbot struck pay dirt. Nobody needed to convince the public that Butterball turkeys tasted good, she said; everybody knew that. The problem was that whole turkeys were intimidating to cook, especially at holiday times, with relatives and friends all around expecting a festive, well-cooked meal. "Turkey trauma," Talbot called it. She suggested a 1-800 hotline that would function just like any other hotline. And so the Butterball Turkey Talk-Line was born.

The campaign started out simply enough. Prior to Thanksgiving 1981, Edelman enlisted the services of a half-dozen experts who would be on hand at Butterball headquarters in Downers Grove, Illinois, to answer questions from harried home cooks. The scheme was an immediate hit. The six experts that first year were flooded with more than 11,000 calls – resulting in an avalanche of media coverage.

The Turkey Talk-Line is now in its third decade, a centerpiece of Butterball's public relations efforts. Over the years, its call staff has mushroomed to 50 dietitians who now handle more than 100,000 questions each November and December. The experts attend "Butterball University" to help them prepare for the onslaught, during which people ask questions about everything from the best thawing techniques to how to put out kitchen fires.

CHAPTER 8

GROWING PAINS, GAINS

From the day Dan founded Edelman, in Chicago, he made efforts to expand the operation to other cities, first to New York, then San Francisco and Los Angeles, next to Washington, D.C., then overseas with offices in London, Frankfurt, and Paris. Now, almost three decades later, circumstances were forcing the firm to shrink.

The loss of the Wine Institute account in 1975 had led to the closing of the San Francisco office. Then, in 1981, John Meek left the firm. The Washington, D.C., office, which Meek had staffed mainly with Democrats, struggled to stay in business following the presidential election of Republican Ronald Reagan. And the new Paris office was losing so much money that it threatened the entire foreign operation; Dan had no choice but to shut it down as well.

In New York, Dan suffered another crippling blow when Warner Cable offered Dick Aurelio a top position that he couldn't refuse. Dan pleaded with him to stay and offered him a substantial raise, but he couldn't match the Warner offer, and Aurelio departed.

This sent Dan scrambling. He first hired an executive from Hill & Knowlton, who proved to be an incompetent leader. The next person fared just as poorly, and Dan had to let him go within a year.

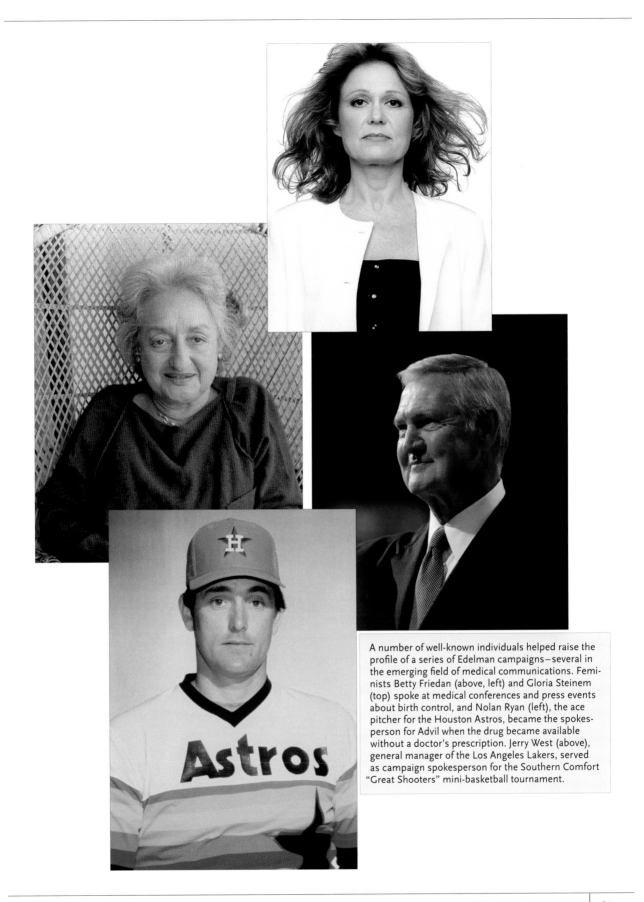

A number of well-known individuals helped raise the profile of a series of Edelman campaigns—several in the emerging field of medical communications. Feminists Betty Friedan (above, left) and Gloria Steinem (top) spoke at medical conferences and press events about birth control, and Nolan Ryan (left), the ace pitcher for the Houston Astros, became the spokesperson for Advil when the drug became available without a doctor's prescription. Jerry West (above), general manager of the Los Angeles Lakers, served as campaign spokesperson for the Southern Comfort "Great Shooters" mini-basketball tournament.

With only his Chicago, Los Angeles, and London offices providing significant profits, Dan was desperate to make the New York operation a success. The future of his company depended on it. He turned to Richard as a last resort. "My father said, 'Why don't you just take a shot at this until I get somebody decent,'" said Richard. "So there I was at the age of 27, the temporary manager of an office with about 15 people, billing less than a couple million dollars a year."

BACK TO HEALTH

The New York office, which Dan had opened in the 1950s to provide media support for the firm's Chicago-based consumer accounts, had matured under Aurelio's leadership, but had never developed specialty areas of its own. Richard saw that he needed to devise a new strategy. "Edelman in the UK had won some health care clients," said Richard. "I thought that was something New York could do well."

Edelman London had started to work for Swiss pharmaceutical giant Hoffmann-La Roche in 1976, several months after an explosion at a company-owned plant in Seveso, Italy, had released a poisonous cloud containing high levels of dioxide into the air. Company officials, criticized for their handling of the crisis, hired Edelman to review and improve the P.R. operations of Hoffmann-La Roche worldwide.

At the same time, the Edelman London office was also helping another Swiss company, Nestlé, prepare for a major World Health Organization conference that would establish standards for marketing infant formulas in developing countries and, with any luck, end the boycott against Nestlé products. Edelman worked side-by-side with a group of infant formula manufacturers, including American Home Products, to hammer out a ban on advertising and sales promotions that discouraged breast-feeding. The contacts

Edelman made through this effort would pay off in the form of health care business in New York.

"I got us on the pitch list for American Home Products for their heart drug Inderal," said Richard. "I contacted a freelance writer from *Drug Topics* magazine named Richard Rothstein, and we wrote the pitch. To our surprise, we won. That was the beginning of the Edelman medical communications practice in the U.S."

Inderal, the brand name of propanolol, was the world's first beta blocker, a drug that revolutionized the treatment of heart disease and became a top seller for American Home Products. The pharmaceutical company tapped Edelman to help spread the word about a new, extended-release Inderal pill. Despite a lack of experience with such campaigns, Richard and Rothstein were able to secure significant media coverage about the new product, including a segment on the *CBS Evening News*.

"But when the CBS reporter called over to American Home Products for a quote, he could only reach a corporate secretary," said Richard. "So when he asked her why the company was offering the new pill, she said, 'Well, it was just one of those things.' And that's the quote CBS used."

EASING THE PAIN

Pleased with Edelman's efforts (including the CBS story), American Home Products reached out to the firm and its nascent medical communications group for public relations help promoting and positioning its ibuprofen pain reliever Advil.

When the Food and Drug Administration approved ibuprofen for over-the-counter sales in 1984, American Home Products found itself in a race with Upjohn and its brand of ibuprofen, Nuprin, to become "first-to-market, best-to-market." At the same, American Home products needed to fend off disparaging comments from the makers

When Advil's advertising firm enlisted Nolan Ryan, seen here between Dan and Richard, to do television commercials, Richard enjoyed reminding him that he was a P.R. spokesman first.

of aspirin, acetaminophen, and other pain relievers that were threatened by the FDA ruling.

Speed was essential. The Edelman campaign quickly spread the word to media, retailers, and consumers that Advil would be shipped to stores the day after receiving FDA approval. Advil zoomed to the top of the category, far ahead of Nuprin, while assuming a large portion of the overall pain reliever market.

"The campaign supporting the Advil prescription-OTC switch established the gold standard not only in prescription-to-OTC switches, but also helped to shape the way we talked to consumers about health in the P.R. world as a whole," said Lisa Sepulveda, an Edelman consumer specialist who spearheaded Advil campaigns for nearly 20 years.

In the months and years that followed, Edelman extolled Advil's many benefits in a succession of creative campaigns. As part of those efforts, Edelman hired Houston Astros ace pitcher Nolan Ryan to become the Advil spokesman. "Nolan did such a good job with our public relations events that Advil's advertising firm enlisted him to do television commercials," said Richard. "I always liked to remind him that he was a P.R. spokesman first."

LINKING HEALTH CARE TO A GREATER SOCIETAL GOOD

"Another early client of the Edelman medical group was Ortho Pharmaceutical at the time of the 25th anniversary of the birth control pill," said Richard. "We thought we could bring creative consumer and corporate responsibility thinking to the health care industry. That was the idea behind our getting well-known feminists Betty Friedan and Gloria Steinem involved."

Ortho had a new birth control pill ready for market – Novum 7/7/7. Instead of just a traditional drug launch, Edelman decided to try to broaden the effort by tying it to the 25th anniversary of the pill, and thereby fostering a discussion about women's reproductive rights. At medical conferences and media events, Friedan and Steinem encouraged doctors to be more open and informative with their patients about birth control.

The two women also urged researchers to pursue work on development of a male birth control pill; it was a controversial position that fueled debate – and media coverage – about reproductive responsibilities. The Edelman campaign, which came at a time when television networks prohibited birth control advertising, helped boost sales of Novum 7/7/7 and allowed Ortho to maintain its status as the nation's top birth control pill manufacturer.

Edelman's campaign for Novum 7/7/7 helped to boost sales of the new pill in the absence of television advertising. At the time, TV ads for contraceptive devices were forbidden.

GO FOR THE GOLD

While the New York office was developing a specialty in health care, the consumer division took a giant step forward with a distinctive campaign for Fuji Film. The work had to do with Fuji's sponsorship role in the 1984 Summer Olympics in Los Angeles, but the pitch to the company's Japanese executives had the makings of a disaster.

"The Fuji executives had their heads bowed during the presentation," said Jody Quinn, who had begun her career at Edelman as a consumer marketing specialist in 1977. "We thought they were asleep. But they were actually listening to what we were saying and silently translating it from English to Japanese to themselves."

As part of the Edelman recommendations, Richard urged the Fuji team to stage a satellite press conference with Chairman Setsutaro Kobayashi, who would appear live from Tokyo. "The only problem was that Chairman Kobayashi had been dead for four years," said Quinn. "But the faux pas had a silver lining. The Fuji president in the U.S. said, 'We thought if a firm could bring Chairman Kobayashi back from the dead, it could do wonders with our Olympic sponsorship.'"

"The presentation didn't go according to plan, but Jody won them over with a brilliant idea," said Richard. Quinn recommended that award-winning *Sports Illustrated* photographer Walter Iooss Jr. use Fuji film to shoot U.S. athletes training for – and then competing in – the L.A. Olympics. The photos would be compiled in a book and also be turned into a touring exhibition to promote the athletes, the Games, and Fuji's new film products. The Fuji executives were so enthralled that they spent the last half of the pitch looking at Iooss's portfolio and talking about his artistic vision for the project.

The effort was "one of those campaigns that unfold exactly according to plan," said Richard. *New York Times* columnist Dave Anderson penned the book's introduction, and the Iooss photos wowed audiences in venues such as the National Geographic Museum in Washington, D.C. After the Games, the Fuji/Edelman relationship continued for 20 years and resulted in dozens of projects.

"That was a seminal account," said Quinn, who remains at Edelman to this day. "The Fuji business saw many industry firsts and helped Edelman gain traction in many practices and sectors – consumer tech, global trade policy, and corporate social responsibility."

SHOOTING FOR SALES

While the Edelman offices had always experienced their share of ups and downs, one

Edelman's campaign for Fuji featured photographs of the 1984 Olympic athletes taken by award-winning *Sports Illustrated* photographer Walter Iooss Jr. on Fuji film.

quality remained constant: creativity. From the Toni Twins on, Dan saw to it that each campaign involved imaginative thinking.

"The great thing about Edelman is that when it came to creativity, there were no holds barred," said George Drucker, a consumer specialist who joined the firm in 1975. "In the late 1970s and '80s, we started to transcend our thinking from traditional P.R. activities into events and promotions that linked directly to sales. This is because more marketing people were questioning the value of publicity. They'd say, 'This is fine, but what has it done aside from boosting awareness?'"

Edelman fine-tuned this new approach – not in boardrooms, but in local bars.

The KFC account had given Edelman a beachhead in Louisville, Kentucky, which in turn helped the firm win an account from the Brown-Forman Corporation to promote its whiskey-flavored liqueur, Southern Comfort. At the time, ads for alcoholic beverages were not allowed on television, so Southern Comfort needed creative ways to boost sales.

Edelman came up with the Southern Comfort "Great Shooters" mini-basketball tournament. In it, patrons in more than 1,000 sports bars across the United States participated in contests involving a Nerf ball and a six-foot-high hoop. Los Angeles Lakers general manager Jerry West was the campaign's spokesman and host of the tournament's championship games in New York; the winner received a trip to the NBA playoffs.

Stirring the competitive spirits of barroom athletes, the campaign continued – and grew – for a decade. Each year, the Edelman team came up with a new twist, including Nerf ball shooting contests featuring NBA legends Rick Barry and Oscar Robertson. And each year Southern Comfort would come up with a drink to go with

the contests. When the mini-basketball tournaments ended, Edelman staged Southern Comfort flick football contests in the same bars at which the tourneys had been held.

"The Southern Comfort brand was up in sales for 10 straight years, and the only thing Brown-Forman did that was different was the contests," said Drucker. "We ended up representing most of the Brown-Forman brands, and doing things like national thumb wrestling contests for Canadian Mist, hosted by former professional wrestler Captain Lou Albano. It was a blast, and everything we did boosted sales."

GOING NUTS

The Edelman consumer campaigns continued to evolve, drawing on Dan's media tour approach, his creativity and encouragement of the "Big Idea," and nationwide events and promotions that tied directly to sales. For Fisher Nuts, an account the agency won as a result of its work for Orville Redenbacher, Edelman launched "America's Nuttiest Sports Nut," a campaign-cum-talent-search.

With bombastic basketball announcer Dick Vitale as host, the search turned up unusual sports fanatics, such as a couple who got married at Candlestick Park (the home field of the San Francisco 49ers), and a Wisconsin nun who listened to Green Bay Packers games on a transistor radio with earphones while singing in the church choir. Finalists were given three minutes to make their case to a panel of celebrity judges in New York. The top prize went to Matthew "Pop" Shortell, a New York Yankees fan who had not missed a game in 50 years.

The success of Great Shooters and America's Nuttiest Sports Nut pushed Edelman into new specialties, including sports marketing. The firm hired former DePaul University athletic director Ed Manetta Jr. to lead its new sports management group. Manetta and his team brought in clients like *Inside Sports* magazine, the Rosemont Horizon sports arena in Chicago, and the Virginia Slims women's professional tennis tour.

The offbeat consumer campaigns also strengthened Edelman's ties to the entertainment industry. The firm staged a Southern Comfort search for America's next top rock band and organized a country music songwriting challenge on behalf of KFC. "Those efforts were the precursor of shows like *American Idol* and *Dancing with the Stars*," said Drucker. "In many ways, it was the birth of reality TV."

SELLING OUT?

Eager to strengthen Edelman's presence in the Golden State, Dan purchased the P.R. arm of Dailey & Associates, a California-based advertising firm with offices in Los Angeles and San Francisco. The deal required Dan to do something he had long resisted: sell part of his firm. In this case, a 5 percent share to the Interpublic Group of Companies, the ad agency conglomerate that was Dailey & Associates' parent.

Dan hated the idea of losing a share of his agency, even though it was only 5 percent. But the deal did allow him to once again have an office in San Francisco and bolster the staff in Los Angeles, which was especially important as the Summer Olympics were coming to town. The Dailey acquisition also added new clients to the Edelman roster, including Honda's motorcycle, scooter, and home generator divisions. Edelman's presence in the Golden State was as strong as it had ever been.

Still, Dan struggled with the partial ownership arrangement, and after a year and a half, he exercised an option he had inserted into the deal that allowed him to buy back the share at book value. Edelman, once again, became 100 percent independent

FAMILY TIES

Following in her father's footsteps, Renée Edelman graduated from Columbia Journalism School, and then joined the staff of the *New York Daily News* as a news assistant. While there, she learned how to edit copy, wrote the occasional feature story, and befriended dozens of New York reporters. She left the paper after more than a year to spend three and a half years as a municipal reporter for *Home News* in New Brunswick, New Jersey.

Renée Edelman graduated from Yale University in 1977. Brothers John (left) and Richard (right) were on hand to celebrate.

In 1985, after she was let go from her next job, as a children's wear editor at *Women's Wear Daily*, Renée received an invitation from her father to join the family firm as an account executive. Her starting salary would be $30,000. Dan told his daughter that she would not receive special treatment ("You'll be one of 500 employees worldwide"), but encouraged her to use her journalism skills and reporter contacts to conduct media relations on behalf of Edelman clients.

Working with Dan and Richard, Renée helped organize a luncheon in New York City in 1988 to mark the 40th anniversary of the media tour that Dan had created with the Toni Twins. The well-attended event featured Charlie Lubin, founder of Sara Lee; Gary Fisk, the grandson of Orville Redenbacher; Morris the Cat and his trainer; and Alva and Alice Anderson, two of the original Toni Twins. For the morning of the luncheon, Renée arranged for her father to appear with the Anderson twins on *The Today Show* with Bob Costas as guest anchor. "My father helped me take my passion for sto-

Dan proudly shows off the fruits of 40 years of creativity, including mementos from the Toni, Brunswick, Morris the Cat, and KFC campaigns.

rytelling, photography, and helping people, and turn it into a career," said Renée.

In 1984, John Edelman graduated from Northwestern University's Kellogg School of Management, where he studied marketing as well as public- and nonprofit-organization management. When Edelman won a contract with the Illinois

Dan and John enjoy a lighthearted moment at John's graduation from the Kellogg School of Management at Northwestern University in 1984.

Department of Commerce and Community Affairs, Dan persuaded John to join the agency and work on the account.

Soon after, wanting John to gain managerial experience, Dan sent him to run a small new office in Dallas, opened after Edelman had won an account with the Mercantile Bank and Trust Company of Texas. In addition to assisting the bank with financial P.R., John oversaw campaigns like the Boy Scouts of America's 75th anniversary celebration, which included an exhibition of Norman Rockwell paintings of scout life that traveled to Los Angeles, New York, and Chicago.

From Day 1 on the job, John gravitated toward nonprofit P.R. work. He helped the Voluntary Hospital Association create a branding program by conducting blood cholesterol screenings at the Dallas-area VHA hospital. In 1988, John left Edelman to take a job with Dallas Can Academy, a group of charter schools that provide education and job training to at-risk youth. Dan never stopped urging his youngest son to rejoin the firm.

A HIDDEN PAIN

By all outward appearances, Ruth Edelman made a smooth transition to "empty-nest" life after her children left for schools and careers. She joined the Chicago office of United States Senator Charles Percy, helping Percy with community events for nearly a decade, adding her personal style and touch to his organization. "I once produced a silk scarf for Chuck with a pattern designed by Halston," said Ruth. "We sold it to raise funds when Chuck was running for reelection."

After her service with Percy, Ruth became special events chair for the state of Illinois under Governor Jim Thompson. Ruth's and Dan's names and photographs regularly found their way into the society pages of Chicago newspapers.

But on the inside, Ruth struggled. She began to skip the parties and fund-raisers, leaving Dan to go it alone. When she could muster the strength to attend these events, Ruth often experienced mood swings. Once, at a dinner party at the Edelman apartment, she fell asleep at the table. She began to put on weight – as much as 40 pounds. Doctors eventually came up with a diagnosis of manic depression.

"I spent seven or eight years almost alone," Ruth told the *Chicago Tribune*. "Manic depression is a very personal disease. It takes a while to adjust to the fact that you have this illness."

Ruth's friend Eppie Lederer (better known as the advice columnist Ann Landers) put her in touch with Dr. Frederick Goodwin, director of the U.S. Alcohol, Drug Abuse and Mental Health

In 1992, Ruth Edelman was photographed by the famed Victor Skrebneski. Her slide into manic depression was just beginning.

Administration. Ruth spent six months in Goodwin's care in Washington, D.C. He prescribed medications, stabilized her condition, and arranged for her care once she returned to Chicago.

Dan, who had helped Ruth hide her illness for many years, now stood beside her as she shared her story. "He never said anything bad about me or my illness, and I love him for it," said Ruth. "Many couples get divorced when one partner is so sick. Dan stood by me during some tough times."

As Ruth regained her mental strength and former physical condition, she decided to put her extensive contacts to use, organizing an annual seminar to educate congressional leaders about mental health. Once, at a mental health charity event in Washington, Ruth and actor Rod Steiger helped raise $40 million for the cause.

In 1994, Ruth received a humanitarian award from the National Depressive and Manic-Depressive Association for her many efforts to raise funds for mental health and help dispel its myths and stigmas.

ASIA RISING

As Ruth hit a new stride, so too did the firm that bore her family's name.

Michael Morley, Edelman's president of international operations, moved to New York in 1984 to better integrate global campaigns, build the firm's expansion abroad, and entice foreign clients like Jaguar Motors to do more public relations in the United States. Morley also moved quickly to reopen an Edelman office in Paris.

On the other side of the globe, Edelman opened its first office in Asia, thanks in large part to the efforts of Jeanette Robertson-Lomax, an adventurous Australian from the Edelman London office. Robertson-Lomax's husband had been transferred to the Malaysian capital, Kuala Lumpur, and rather than lose her as an employee, Dan and Morley asked her to explore opportunities in her new country.

"She found an entrepreneur who owned an ad agency in Kuala Lumpur and also had an interest in a P.R. company in Singapore," said Morley. "We did a deal that gave us control of the Kuala Lumpur firm and a significant interest in the one in Singapore."

Another Robertson-Lomax deal established an Edelman office in Hong Kong, and about the same time Edelman opened an office in Sydney. The agency suddenly had a strong presence in that part of the world.

TAKING OFF

In New York, Morley's responsibility was not only to build the international network, but also direct large accounts with a global reach. Soon after the American bombing raid on Libya in April 1986, Edelman had such an opportunity. With transatlantic air travel plummeting due to fears of retaliatory terrorism, British Air reached out to Edelman for an emergency P.R. effort to restore consumer confidence.

Within one week, Edelman mobilized 10 offices and affiliates to stage an $8 million campaign called "Go for It America," which flew 5,200 Americans to London and back free of charge. Grand prizes included a $100,000 shopping spree at Harrods department store and a five-year lease on a London town house. Edelman also arranged for a select group of American visitors to have tea at No. 10 Downing Street with Prime Minister Margaret Thatcher.

Journalists from both sides of the Atlantic hopped onto the flights, covering the winners and reporting on the festivities. The media attention helped double airline bookings, leading analysts to call it the most successful promotion in aviation history.

For Edelman, the campaign also strengthened coordination between the U.S. and European offices, giving the entire agency a boost. "It was a very public program and thus was top of mind for everyone, not just the media," said Morley. "All other clients and prospects knew about it, especially in the airline industry. It was instrumental in our landing, so to speak, the Continental Airlines, SAS, and Amadeus accounts in subsequent months and years."

Dan felt a renewed confidence about his firm's ability to profit and expand abroad.

AN ENVIRONMENTAL FIRST

Following the departure of John Meek in 1981, Dan struggled for eight years to staff the Edelman office in Washington, D.C., with the right people. In 1986, he purchased Jean Rainey and Associates, a small, D.C.-based firm that specialized in food P.R. and handled work for such clients as the sugar manufacturing trade organization. Staffers joked that the acquisition gave the operation a "sugar high." Dan knew the office still needed a few high-level public affairs experts to shape it into one of the town's leading agencies. He asked Richard to take over the effort.

Leslie Dach joined Edelman to run global public affairs and would establish the firm as a leader in environmental P.R.

Through John Scanlon, Richard approached Leslie Dach, who had been communications director for the Michael Dukakis presidential campaign as well as a lobbyist for the National Audubon Society and the Environmental Defense Fund. He offered the affable Dach a job in the D.C. office heading the company's global public affairs practice. Within months of joining the firm, Dach helped Edelman unveil one of its most influential campaigns – an effort that blended the best of the firm's consumer, environmental, and public affairs capabilities.

In 1989, the H.J. Heinz Company, owner of the StarKist tuna brand, approached Edelman to help make an announcement. In response to a chorus of complaints from environmentalists and a growing consumer boycott brought about by the fact that tuna fishing nets accidentally resulted in the death of up to 100,000 dolphins annually, Heinz had devised a new way to fish for tuna that would spare dolphins. The company, which supplied one-third of the world's canned tuna, called its new product Dolphin Safe Tuna.

With Pam Talbot leading the consumer division efforts in Chicago, Dach orchestrating public affairs support from Washington, D.C., and the Los Angeles office coordinating endorsements from the entertainment industry, Edelman helped Heinz reshape the entire industry. The company arranged for Heinz to partner with the influential Earth Island Institute as well as environmentally active Hollywood celebrities like Ted Danson and Tom Cruise. It also worked with Congress to make sure Dolphin Safe Tuna became the industry standard.

Within hours of the Heinz announcement, the second and third largest tuna suppliers – Van Camp Seafood (Chicken of the Sea) and Bumble Bee – announced dolphin-safe policies of their own. Heinz had gone from boycott target to environmental role model.

Dan reveled in the work, buoyed by the way his offices and personnel worked together. His firm had carried out a new form of environmental public relations, a practice that was sure to grow in the approaching decade of the '90s and beyond.

"The Dolphin Safe Tuna campaign really established Edelman as a leader in environmental public relations," said Leslie Dach. "It helped the firm create a new type of practice where Edelman could help businesses and environmental organizations work together for the betterment of the environment and company bottom lines."

LIKE FATHER, LIKE SON

Everywhere Dan looked, he saw reasons to be optimistic. Richard, Jody Quinn, Richard Rothstein, and others had shaped the New York office into a profit center to rival Edelman Chicago. Leslie Dach and staff had restored Edelman D.C. to prominence. Pam Talbot was proving to be the most talented public relations executive Dan had ever hired. Edelman was back in business in San Francisco and greatly strengthened in Los Angeles, thanks to Tom Harrison and company. Michael Morley had not only reopened an office in Paris, but also set up a string of offices in Asia and was looking to establish many more outposts around the globe.

Richard's career – and life – mirrored his father's at about the same age. He had moved to a new city and built a business through hard work, new contacts, and out-of-the-box thinking. Like his father, Richard took full advantage of his new city's social offerings, only to change course when the right woman came along.

"I was at a party, and I saw Roz," said Richard. "I thought she was cute. I waited for her boyfriend to get a drink so I could get her phone number. As it turned out, I didn't get the number, but I got her name and found out where she worked. So I called her at her office the next day."

Richard and Rosalind Walrath on their wedding day.

Richard Edelman married Rosalind Walrath at the Harvard Club in Manhattan on May 17, 1986. John Edelman served as his brother's best man. Roz kept her maiden name and continued to work as an investment banker in New York. The newlyweds honeymooned in China.

Then, in a scene that might have been lifted directly from Dan's early days in the business, Richard arrived at work one day in the late 1980s to discover that a large contingent of his employees had left to join a competitor, taking some of the health care business with them. As his father had done in similar circumstances all those years before, Richard found himself scrambling to hold the office together.

"We kept most of the accounts, and I ran them myself," Richard said. "We rebuilt our health practice. And in the process I learned about the importance of having people sign non-compete agreements."

YES, DO TALK TO STRANGERS

"When I was a boy, I used to ride on the train from Chicago to Milwaukee with my dad," said John Edelman. "He'd point to the names of companies on the billboards and say, 'I'm going to give them a cold call.'"

When Richard became general manager of the New York office, he adopted the approach as well.

"Not knowing anything about office management, I just started cold calling potential clients," said Richard. "I called up this guy at Unilever, and they gave us a chance on a new product launch for Surf detergent. And we won."

"An even better campaign for Unilever was our campaign for Snuggle fabric softener," said Richard. "Snuggle the Bear became the official 'spokesbear' for Reading Is Fundamental, the nation's leading nonprofit children's literacy organization. We organized numerous reading events at libraries with kids and Snuggle the Bear. The campaign was a huge hit. And it all came from a cold call."

Dan's practice of reaching out to potential clients rubbed off on his daughter, too.

"My father met a lot of clients on airplanes," said Renée. "He'd come back from trips with business cards and ask Richard or other employees to follow up. I learned to talk to people on airplanes because of him. You never know who you are going to meet."

CHAPTER 9

OVER THE WALL

After Edelman reached its 40th anniversary, Dan Edelman's decision to keep his public relations agency independent and privately owned drew criticism from industry watchers and competitors.

Public relations firms owned by advertising agencies still towered over Edelman, winning business by offering clients a so-called "whole egg" approach to marketing – advertising, P.R., direct mail, and sales promotion. Dan was now 72. Analysts doubted his ability to compete for the top spot, pointing to the fact that Edelman had been in business for decades, yet had never cracked P.R.'s top echelon, which included Burson-Marsteller and Hill & Knowlton.

"We've been as high as five," said Dan, ruefully, in an interview with *PR Week* in 1989. "But new things come along – like Shandwick from nowhere, and Saatchi and Ogilvy." He wondered whether his independent strategy would ever propel his firm to match the others.

On top of that, he grew frustrated watching other P.R. firms race ahead of his to plant flags in key places around the globe. "We recognize we must be able to compete internationally, said Dan in the same interview. "But we recognize we don't have the unlimited resources of, say, a large multinational ad agency with a P.R. arm or a Shandwick-style holding company. We don't have all the money in the world, so we can't just go out to Japan or even Scotland and buy the best and most expensive consultancy in that country."

Marketing
IRELAND'S MARKETING MONTHLY
VOLUME 2, NO. 5   MAY/JUNE 1991

PR SPECIAL:
Edelman eager
to expand

With his firm still eclipsed by the top echelon, Dan continued to push for international expansion, particularly in Asia. He traveled to Tokyo in 1986; was rendered galloping around the globe in a cartoon sketched by staff members; held the firm's 1996 global leadership meeting in Hong Kong; spoke out in one of many interviews; and took time with son Richard to celebrate the media tour's 40th anniversary.

Dan opted for a conservative approach to overseas expansion, preferring to open an office from scratch or merge with a smaller, less expensive firm, financing all moves out of retained earnings. Although he didn't have the buying power of the advertising conglomerates, he could act quickly and pay with cash.

Increasingly, Dan saw the future of P.R. growing most rapidly on foreign soil. If he was ever going to catch the leading firms, he would need to do so abroad, especially in Asia, where his agency lagged far behind giants like Shandwick and Burson-Marsteller. In 1992, Shandwick earned $24.5 million in the Asia Pacific region, while Edelman grossed just $3 million.

Asia was a race Dan needed to win. He renamed his business Edelman Public Relations Worldwide and set his sights eastward.

"ONE OF THE GREAT DISAPPOINT- MENTS IN MY CAREER"

"In 1984, I forged a partnership with Hakuhodo in Tokyo, the second largest ad agency in Japan," said Dan, years later. "We had agreed on a joint venture arrangement without any exchange of funds. I still have the pictures on the wall in our Chicago office of the meeting with Chairman Kondo and President Isobe.

"The meeting was followed by a luncheon at a Tokyo club. There was extensive general business page and trade publicity. I spoke with suitable translation to well over 100 of their public relations executives. I thought I was on a great ride that would enable us to become the lead firm in Japan."

Over the coming months, Edelman referred business to Hakuhodo, but received very little in return. "It was one of the great disappointments in my career that this arrangement never became a reality."

Frustrated, Dan asked Hakuhodo to let him out of the deal so he could pursue another partnership with a large Japanese public relations firm.

"The founder and CEO hosted a big reception for me at one of the leading Tokyo hotels with 200 or 300 people on hand," said Dan. "There were huge signs on the walls dramatizing the link

Michael Morley and Dan Edelman (standing, left and right) and Richard Edelman (bottom, center) with top executives from Hakuhodo before the relationship with the Japanese agency soured.

between Edelman and this firm. Once again, I was on a high and once again, I was totally let down. Nothing at all happened. The CEO was interested only in working with Japanese clients in Japan. We referred some U.S. business to his firm but it wasn't handled well."

So Dan ended that partnership as well, and instead launched a start-up Edelman office in Tokyo. The new operation got off to a bad start.

"We had to move when we discovered through an old friend in Tokyo that we were in the 'fish market' area," said Dan. "I also was forced to drop a nonperforming manager. The next manager took care of the office location problem by moving us into a high-rise office building just behind the Okura Hotel. The rent was staggering. We flailed for a few years and had to close the office."

The Tokyo hemorrhaging threatened the entire Asian operation, but not Dan's resolve.

"Though we put aside thoughts about Japan at that time, I wasn't going to be stalled in my commitment to put roots down all around Asia," said Dan. "I knew we'd go back to Japan later." Asia, he believed, would soon drive the world economy and determine which P.R. firm would become the world's largest.

OVER THE WALL

While Japan proved difficult on many levels, China was an ideal fit for Dan and his agency. In China, public relations was just coming into its own, just as it had in America when Dan started his firm. Edelman's strengths meshed with China's most lucrative markets and greatest needs, including consumer, health care, and public affairs. The firm's clients, eager to expand their businesses in the world's largest country, pressed Dan to open an operation in China.

The question was not if or when Edelman should enter China, but how. Dan feared a repeat of his Tokyo experience. He swore he would avoid a similar fate. In a twist, the ideal partner approached him.

Founded in the mid-1980s and managed by French entrepreneur Serge Dumont, Interasia Communications was the first and largest independent P.R. firm on the Chinese mainland at the time, with offices in Beijing, Shanghai, and Guangzhou. By 1993, nearly every top 10 international public relations agency had approached Dumont to inquire about purchasing his firm.

"Edelman was the one firm that didn't contact me," said Dumont. "But the more I looked at Edelman, the more commonality I saw. We were both entrepreneurs, independent, pioneering, ethical, client-focused, and with ambitious long-term goals for the future. So I reached out to Dan."

Dumont met Dan for an introductory dinner at the Mandarin Hotel in Hong Kong. They hit it off from the start, sharing their views of the public relations profession and dreams for its development in Asia. "I could see that Dan had a genuine interest and passion for China," said Dumont.

Dan and Dumont struck a deal for Edelman to purchase Interasia. Overnight, Edelman became the leading public relations presence in China, with 35 staffers in three offices. Clients included Mars, Kodak, Compaq Computer, DuPont, Hennessy, Christian Dior, and Kentucky Fried Chicken. China became Edelman's Asia hub.

There was only one snag. The Chinese business name for Edelman could also be translated to mean "slow lover" or "loving slowly." "There was a long pause after I called Dan to tell him the 'slow lover' news," said Dumont. "Then he laughed and said, 'Well, Serge, what can we expect at my age?'" The Edelman name – and its translation – stuck.

When Edelman acquired Interasia, it became the leading P.R. firm in China. Dan, Serge Dumont, and the Beijing team wave from the Temple of Heaven in celebration of the new Edelman office.

Children, dressed up like KFC's Colonel Sanders, were part of the festivities in Shanghai that marked the opening of the restaurant chain's 9,000th store worldwide.

"In Beijing, we want to enter the market for public relations on behalf of government organizations and large enterprises," said Dan in announcing the new Edelman China operation. "In Shanghai, we want to develop P.R. activities for consumer products promotions. In Guangzhou province near Hong Kong, we are thinking of more marketing-oriented, more Western-style business."

He and Dumont also aimed to change the practice of paying Chinese journalists for coverage, arguing that if the firm and others didn't take a stand, pay-for-print would remain the modus operandi in China. The cutoff of funds rankled many reporters at first, but soon became the industry norm. Dumont also spearheaded an effort to get the top international P.R. firms operating in China to adopt additional ethical standards, such as strict limits on gifts, meals, and trips.

The new Edelman operation spent a significant amount of time educating Chinese business leaders on the types of P.R. campaigns that would help them obtain investors in the United States and elsewhere. The agency pushed Chinese companies to open up their operations and finances, while encouraging Chinese executives to curtail their fondness for making long speeches.

On behalf of KFC, Edelman organized a massive chicken dance on the riverfront Bund in Shanghai in 1994, featuring hundreds of children dressed like Colonel Sanders to celebrate KFC's opening of its 9,000th store worldwide. Edelman also won the Procter & Gamble P.R. business in China.

By the end of 1994, more than one-third of all Edelman revenues originated abroad; *PR News* named Dan Edelman "P.R. Professional of the Year." The 72-year-old "father of modern public relations" still had much to show the P.R. world.

MORE FOREIGN FLAGS

Edelman didn't limit its growth to China and Asia in the early 1990s. Dan bought a small firm in Dublin with expertise in financial and health care P.R. He and Michael Morley also opened offices in Milan, Brussels, and Madrid.

Calling the '90s the "golden age of public relations," Dan predicted the industry would continue to grow its way out of the recession that was gripping much of the world. While P.R. firms owned by advertising agencies continued to outpace his own, Dan publicly predicted independence would pay off in the long run. Conglomerate agencies ultimately would sacrifice quality and resources to meet stockholder demands, he argued. Few believed him.

Edelman continued its measured approach. "We're not trying to swallow elephants," said Dan to *PR Week*. "We only take small bites. So if an office doesn't work out, it won't be a major blow."

The strategy paid off in Canada, where Edelman had purchased the Houston Group, with offices in Montreal and Toronto, in 1991. When founder Stan Houston became ill, Edelman hired Molson executive Charles Fremes to turn the business around.

Dan argued that the greatest threat to the public relations industry was not the economy, but the practices of some leading firms. Citing P.R. campaigns on behalf of the Church of Scientology and the government of Kuwait during the 1990 Gulf War, Dan argued that all agencies needed to do a better job picking clients.

"I've been concerned that with the greater power and recognition of public relations, there's been a weakening of the integrity, honesty, and ethical practice," he told the *St. Louis Post-Dispatch*. "Public relations firms have agreed to defend the indefensible."

In speeches to universities and Public Relations Society of America (PRSA) chapters throughout the country, Dan advocated better recruitment by P.R. agencies, more public relations classes and majors, greater PRSA involvement, and higher industry standards. His advocacy and honesty did not win him many friends in the industry.

DOMESTIC GROWTH

While foreign acquisitions and office openings garnered most of the headlines, American offices figured equally into Dan's expansion plans. Edelman opened offices in Atlanta and St. Louis, as well as in Silicon Valley and Sacramento. His plans to expand in California surprised industry watchers, as the Golden State had been hammered by a string of blows, including a crippling recession and the Los Angeles riots.

Encouraging the moves was a native Californian and Edelman's most high-profile employee, Michael Deaver, former deputy chief of staff to President Ronald Reagan. Once one of the most powerful men in Washington, D.C., Deaver had been convicted of perjury in 1987 for lying to Congress about his lobbying activities. He entered a treatment program for alcoholism and struggled to keep his wife from leaving him.

Dan was introduced to Deaver by Christopher Ogden, then the Washington, D.C., bureau chief for *Time* magazine. Minutes after meeting Deaver, Dan knew he would be a huge asset to the firm. Dan saw a brilliant communicator who had arranged Reagan's most memorable public appearances, including events at Normandy Beach to mark the 40th anniversary of D-Day, and in front of the Berlin Wall, where the president urged Soviet leader Mikhail Gorbachev to "Tear down this wall." Dan recognized that Deaver was a master at taking a complex issue and presenting it to the public in a highly visual, easy-to-understand way.

Dan paired him with Democrat Leslie Dach in the Washington, D.C., office, and new business skyrocketed. Taking advantage of a Rolodex packed with the names of foreign leaders and American captains of industry, Deaver helped Edelman land a string of heavyweight clients, including Boeing, the World Bank, and the governments of Portugal, Chile, and India. Edelman's work on behalf of AT&T and a coalition of long-distance telephone service providers fighting the cable companies over controversial deregulation legislation in Congress significantly raised the firm's profile in town.

"Both Dan and Richard have this ability to convince wildly overqualified people to work for them," said Dach.

Deaver, having scaled Washington's highest heights and suffered its most harrowing depths, brought to Edelman a healthy perspective on life and work. He was happy to stay in the background, while promoting the efforts of young staffers who soaked up his counsel. Interns and junior associates would regularly visit his office for advice on client work or personal matters.

When Edelman had the opportunity to bid on a unique, global account, Deaver was the obvious choice to lead the effort. He gathered a group of Edelman public affairs experts to pitch the Church of Jesus Christ of Latter Day Saints, which wanted help dispelling myths about its practices and beliefs.

"You have such an impressive worldwide communications network, I feel like I'm bringing coals to Newcastle," said Deaver in his pitch to the Mormon elders in Salt Lake City. He and the team then outlined a comprehensive program that encouraged the LDS Church, as it was referred to, to open up and better connect with the public through media, community events, and its upcoming 150th anniversary.

"That was a wonderful presentation," said future LDS President Gordon Hinckley. Then he turned to Dan, who was participating in the presentation. "But let me ask you something, Mr. Edelman. How do you, a Jewish man, feel about representing our faith?"

All eyes darted to Dan, who rose slowly from his chair and buttoned his suit coat. "I'm glad you asked that question," he said. "My grandfather was a rabbi, and my father was a religious scholar. I've long seen our religions as kindred souls, having to wage the same battles over intolerance and misperception. As a Jewish man, I would be honored to fight those battles alongside you."

Edelman represented the LDS Church for the next dozen years, arranging for President Hinckley and other leaders to appear on national talk shows and influential public affairs forums for the first time in the church's history. The agency worked with the church to organize a reenactment of the 1846-47 covered wagon pilgrimage

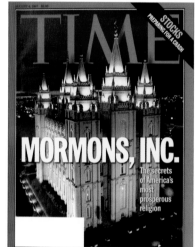

Edelman and the Church of Jesus Christ of Latter Day Saints worked together for more than 10 years.

the Mormons made from Nauvoo, Illinois, to Salt Lake City. The reenactment was featured in a *Time* magazine cover story ("Mormons, Inc.") and in hundreds of media outlets around the world.

The LDS leadership even agreed to appear in a feature story on *60 Minutes* with reporter Mike Wallace. Dan and Richard argued heatedly over the decision, with the elder Edelman fearing that his client would be the target of a hatchet job.

"Well, what happened," said Wallace to Utah's *Deseret News*, "was that my *60 Minutes* colleagues and I learned, from the time we spent with Gordon Hinckley and his wife, from his staff, and from other Mormons who talked to us, that this warm and thoughtful and decent and optimistic leader of the Mormon Church fully deserves the almost universal admiration that he gets."

NEW GROUND IN NEW YORK

Under Richard's leadership, Edelman New York became the firm's leading profit center outside of Chicago. The New York office continued to increase its specialty areas and pioneer new approaches to public relations. Richard led new forays into financial P.R., though the firm's new business sometimes came with mysterious beginnings.

"Michael Morley and I were summoned to a seedy midtown Manhattan hotel for a sit-down with two gentlemen in trench coats," said Richard. "We thought they were either going to expose themselves, or that they worked for the CIA. They asked us about Edelman, in particular our global experience.

The mysterious interrogators turned out to be executives at accounting and consulting giant Ernst & Whinney, which was in the middle of a highly secretive merger with Arthur Young to create Ernst & Young, the largest professional services firm in the world.

After working in secret for six weeks, Edelman rolled out a two-phased campaign. First it explained the merger's rationale to the thousands of employee partners who would need to approve it. Then it made the announcement to the media and clients of the giant new firm. The work became a blueprint for a string of soon-to-follow mergers among accounting and professional services firms.

The work opened more opportunities on Wall Street, where Edelman lagged behind other public relations agencies. The firm worked around the clock on behalf of Viacom CEO Sumner Redstone in his efforts to buy Paramount. When business mogul Barry Diller jumped in with a competing offer, Edelman handled the public relations surrounding a series of counterbids by Viacom, including Redstone's pivotal decision to add Blockbuster to the mix. Once Viacom finalized the purchase, analysts called it the "Deal of the Decade."

"We'd worked all night at Viacom, then we walk to our office in Times Square at sunrise, seeing the headlines and stories about our work in all the newspaper stands," said Richard. "It was a great adrenaline rush."

COMBINING SCIENCE WITH P.R.

The Edelman Medical group continued to grow in revenue, scope of work, and range of clients. In 1994, Richard changed the name to Edelman Healthcare to reflect the division's widening focus.

When Schering-Plough won approval to sell its non-sedating antihistamine, Claritin, it wanted something more substantive than a traditional publicity effort to differentiate the drug from the handful of others in the field. Instead of staging events, Edelman helped the pharmaceutical company conduct an extensive study that examined the differences in productivity and cognitive function between people who took Claritin and those who used Benadryl-type drugs.

"We worked with a university to conduct the study, and it had really strong results," said Nancy Turett, who had taken over the leadership of Edelman Healthcare after Richard Rothstein left the firm. "It showed that if you used a non-sedating antihistamine, you could improve worker productivity. It was a good example of Edelman combining public relations and science into something transactional."

That science-heavy approach continued with the launch of another drug, Searle's sleep medication Ambien. The company had entered a distressed market that was being hampered by side effect fears and widespread stigmas.

For more than a year before Ambien was brought to market, Searle and Edelman conducted a research effort into insomnia – titled Sleep in America. It was the first such study of its kind. The research found dramatic differences between people who have trouble sleeping and people who don't. To gain attention for the study, Edelman published an elegantly produced book called *Mysteries of the Night* that featured the study's findings along with paintings about sleep from artists like Van Gogh and Matisse.

"One of our strategies in much of our pioneering work in our health business has been showing the upsides of treating something, not just how it's going to reduce the downsides," said Turett. "So instead of how bad insomnia is, we made it about how great sleep is. The art helped make that point."

In the 1990s, Edelman Healthcare's campaigns for drug companies began to take on a wellness-first flavor. With Searle, the maker of sleep aid Ambien, Edelman conducted Sleep in America, a research effort into the little understood subject of sleep. Edelman showcased the findings in an illustrated publication called *Mysteries of the Night*.

The results of the survey and book, promoted by Edelman for two years, helped push Ambien to the top of the market, while dispelling stereotypes of sleep medications and encouraging millions to seek help for their sleep problems.

THE POWER OF A CHILD'S IMAGINATION

While Edelman developed new areas of P.R. expertise, its consumer campaigns continued to take fresh, creative approaches, including ones that tapped into the dreams of children.

In 1994, Edelman created Visa Olympics of the Imagination on behalf of the credit card giant. The program invited children from all around the world to submit artwork depicting Olympic themes. Children with the best entries were invited to attend the Summer or Winter Games.

The program clicked from the very beginning, and Visa has extended the Edelman effort to every Summer and Winter Olympics since. Visa Olympics of the Imagination has received millions of submissions and sent thousands of children to the Games to cheer the competition and spread the Olympic spirit.

In a similar vein, in 1995, Edelman staged a nationwide Imagine the Magic competition for Microsoft that asked children to complete the sentence: "The coolest computer could _____." More than 18,000 kids in grades 3 through 6 sent Microsoft chairman Bill Gates ideas, suggesting everything from computers that could do household chores to ones that could help solve homelessness and environmental problems.

Six winners and their parents were flown to Seattle and taken to Microsoft headquarters in Redmond, Washingtson, for a Kids' Technology Summit. They were given Microsoft ID badges and spent some time discussing their ideas with software designers, capping the visit with a private luncheon and joint interview with Gates for *The Today Show*. In later years, the Imagine the Magic program was expanded to India.

VIVA MEXICO

"One of the happiest days of my father's career was when Edelman won the Mexico Tourism account in 1991," said John Edelman. "He loved the work and loved beating out all the other big P.R. agencies for the campaign."

Edelman secured an invitation to compete for the Mexico account thanks to its work on behalf of the National Tour Association, an organization that promotes motor coach tourism throughout North America. The Edelman travel team, led by founder and current head of the firm's Travel and Hospitality practice, Cathleen Johnson, had strengthened the firm's tourism credentials earlier in 1991 after winning a public relations contract to promote Illinois tourism, an account that lasted for the next two decades. Together, these three large accounts, building on the international work led by Michael Morley with clients such as British Airways, established Edelman as a serious contender in global travel P.R.

Johnson remembers the time well. "We were rehearsing in a filmmaker's studio in Mexico City prior to the pitch," said Johnson. "The studio had a funky 1970s décor, with black walls and bean-bag chairs. Dan, in his Brooks Brothers suit and Hermès tie, had joined us there for a serious critique of our upcoming presentation. But the only place he could sit was on a giant red velvet chair shaped like a hand. He had a good laugh over that, and I'll never forget that image."

After a yearlong international public relations effort that helped to double tourist travel to Mexico, Edelman won a landmark two-year, $10 million campaign extension to continue its efforts, making Mexico Tourism the firm's largest account to date. The new campaign, which involved 12 Edelman offices around the world, promised even more promotional activities, including a unique program rarely used in tourism at the time: an interactive computer system. Edelman subsequently won another three-year contract, which included substantial crisis work during a serious outbreak of crime in Mexico.

THE CHICAGO FLOOD

"One of my favorite P.R. moments from the 1990s came one year when I was home in Chicago for Passover," said Richard. "A friend from a private equity firm called me and said Edelman had to help a company embroiled in a local crisis."

The crisis was the Chicago flood of April 13, 1992. The company, Great Lakes Dredge & Dock, was a private dredging contractor that had been hired by the city to drive protective pilings into the Chicago River near the Kinze Street bridge. During the job, dredge workers accidentally punctured an old, 47-mile network of freight tunnels, causing massive flooding to basements in the downtown Loop area and resulting in an estimated $1 billion worth of property damage and business losses.

"Everyone was pointing the finger at this dredging company," said Richard. "They were looking at multimillion-dollar lawsuits and stood a good chance of going out of business."

Richard began the assignment by digging through the dredging company's paperwork for the job, asking if the city had provided a map. Company officials handed him the map they had been given. It did not include any markings or references to the tunnel network. Knowing that cable television companies used the tunnels to string cable, other Edelman staffers hurried to the city department that oversees cable operators and located a detailed map that did include the tunnels.

"So we had a press conference on Saturday morning, where we held up copies of the two maps and let the media know that the dredging company had been given the wrong one," said Richard. "The Chicago papers ran front-page stories the next day, and the blame instantly went to the city. It was great P.R. jujitsu!"

CHAPTER 10

EDELMAN PLUGS IN

To understand the difference between Dan's and Richard's management styles, observers needed to look no further than the desks of the two men. Dan's was piled high with folders, newspaper clippings, and correspondence. It was a lopsided skyline on the brink of crashing to the floor; yet he knew in an instant the location of every document. Dan preferred a wheel-shaped management structure, with all the office managers reporting directly to him. His desk was the cluttered hub.

On the other hand, Richard's desk, in New York, looked like a vacant lot, free of stacks of paper and clutter. He was quicker to delegate and hand papers back to staffers. With his Harvard Business School background, Richard had adopted a pyramid management structure, with managers operating in a hierarchy.

There was another noticeable difference on Richard's desk – a desktop PC. Short emails were perfect for his rapid-fire approach. Dan, meanwhile, eschewed the machines. His secretary, Alice Manheim, would print his emails and hand them to him; he would then dictate responses or pen replies using Flair felt-tip pens.

The 70-year-old former journalist and the MBA son approached the craft of public relations from different perspectives. These were sometimes complementary, sometimes at odds, yet both had been able to expand the business. By the beginning of the 1990s, New York had surpassed Chicago as the agency's

Before Dan handed over the reins of the company to Richard, he ensured that his son had ample international experience. The two are pictured here in Canada.

leading revenue center, and Dan believed that Richard had the skills necessary to lead Edelman in future years.

But before turning over the firm to his eldest off-spring, Dan needed to be sure Richard could oversee multiple offices and manage a multinational region. The opportunity presented itself in 1992, when David Davis, vice chairman and general manager of Edelman in Europe, left the firm. Dan named Richard as Davis's replacement. The job would test the younger Edelman's skills as never before.

To complicate matters, Richard's wife, Roz, was on a fast track at the investment banking firm where she worked, and was bringing in more money than Richard. She couldn't move to Europe. The couple also had two young daughters, six-year-old Margot and two-year-old Victoria (Tory). Richard would have to commute weekly to Europe.

His learning curve was steep and immediate. At the time, Edelman had offices in Dublin, Frankfurt, London, Madrid, Milan, and Paris. After a detailed performance review, Richard discovered that the European division was losing approximately $1 million a year. The London office had just lost a large account with British Steel and would soon lose another major account, the British National Dairy Council. Richard realized that he would need to close some offices and open others in more profitable locations.

Meanwhile, Richard opened an office in Brussels, acquired P.R. firms in Germany and France to bolster Edelman's presence in those countries, and hired Abel Hadden, a well-known British communications practitioner, to run the Edelman London office.

To draw attention to AIDS prevention on behalf of client Benetton, Edelman had the obelisk in Paris's Place de la Concorde covered in a pink sheath to resemble a giant condom. Police removed the covering within hours, but not before it had caught the attention of media the world over.

He urged the European offices to increase their creativity levels. So when Marie Rouet, president of Edelman Paris, and photographer Oliviero Toscani had a seemingly wild idea for their client Benetton to focus attention on AIDS prevention in France, Richard was all for it. Thus, at dawn on December 1, 1993, World AIDS Day, a group of Parisian activists scaled the famous 75-foot Egyptian obelisk in the center of the Place de la Concorde and draped it with a giant pink cloth shaped to look like a condom; it had a small Benetton logo on the side. Police removed the covering an hour or so later, but not before French journalists had captured the spectacle with photographs and videos that appeared in media outlets around the world.

Despite his eagerness to shake up the operation, Richard learned that American ways of doing business did not always mesh with European approaches. For instance, when he attempted to fire the manager of the money-losing Madrid office,

Pam Talbot, who started at Edelman as an account executive, would spend nearly four decades at the firm and lead many of its iconic campaigns. She approached the burgeoning technology business with the eye and skill of a consumer marketer, which she did on behalf of Microsoft.

Edelman attorneys informed him that he would still have to pay her salary for two more years. He closed the office instead.

After seeing what Richard was doing in Europe, there were outsiders who wondered if he had the necessary management skills to someday lead Edelman. "Some former employees and industry experts say that Richard Edelman's aggressive emphasis on financial goals and growth has its drawbacks, resulting in employee turnover they deem to be excessive and inadequate servicing of some clients," reported *The New York Times* in 1994.

In the same *Times* article, John Graham, then the chief executive of Fleishman-Hillard, characterized Edelman as primarily a consumer publicity firm and wondered if Richard was the right person to succeed Dan. "It's going to be a very interesting transition," Graham was quoted as saying. Richard stashed a copy of the article in his desk for inspiration and continued to overhaul Edelman Europe.

He also began to advocate for the use of a new tool that would dramatically alter the practice of public relations and the fortunes of the firm.

THE INTERNET ARRIVES

"One of the great strengths of Edelman is the willingness to recognize disruptive moments – and to run toward them," said Pam Talbot. "Somewhere in the soul of the company is a renegade streak that thrives on the line between the current and the about-to-be. For instance, touring the Toni Twins wasn't just a clever idea. It was also a recognition that the world was moving toward and being moved by images and voices more than words in print. Dan had the courage to use television and an understanding of what would play on the tube."

Now, in the early 1990s, as companies and other organizations began to explore the possibilities of the Internet, Edelman faced an even greater sea change in communications. Most public relations firms and ad agencies reacted to the new communications vehicle with caution. They had little to no web experience and were worried about their ability to control messages in the new medium. Those who did embrace the Internet saw it mostly as a complement to traditional P.R. or advertising campaigns.

Richard had embraced computers from an early age. My first experience with computers goes back to 1968 in Chicago," said Richard. "My school, the Latin School, had an early-model computer. I remember doing punch cards, writing simple programs. I wasn't any kind of programmer, but I was always around computers at school. When I was at Harvard, I did some computer work for my senior project."

Edelman New York had formed a small technology division in 1986, primarily to market new products. The group helped clients like Micron Technology, Data General, NYNEX Mobile Communications, and Hughes LAN Systems unveil their latest offerings. For Samsung Electronics America, Edelman promoted the company's new home security robot, Scout-About, and managed to get the device onto network talk shows. In Australia, Edelman oversaw the product release of Lotus Notes; and in Europe it guided the public launch of the British Telecom Mobile Communications division.

"I remember organizing trade show appearances for the Commodore VIC-20 computer in 1982. That was big deal back then," said Richard. "It was an early PC and a simple arcade-type gaming device that you hooked up to your television, but it gave us all a glimpse into the future of personal computing. That was our first new, emerging tech company.

"It was a great account . . . until Commodore CEO Jack Tramiel fired us after a sign fell during a press conference we had organized," Richard said with a laugh. "He rehired us the following Monday." The VIC-20, the first personal computer to sell more than a million units, was discontinued in 1985.

Edelman built a growing roster of technology clients, but remained on the periphery of the

In the early 1980s, Edelman helped Commodore – one of the firm's first technology clients – market its VIC-20 home computer. The firm's tech roster would grow rapidly after the establishment of a formal technology practice in 1994.

business. But that changed in 1994 when the firm took a number of steps that would shake up the P.R. field and position the company on a new higher-trajectory course.

"Sometimes you get lucky," said Talbot. "And every once in a while you use that luck to build a future."

SILICON VALLEY STRENGTH

When Richard approached IBM's P.R. director, Paul Bergevin, in 1994 asking him to head Edelman's technology division, Bergevin's response was direct. "You don't have a real technology division," he said. "That's why I want you to do it," replied Richard.

Bergevin accepted the assignment and relocated with his family to Silicon Valley, where a small Edelman office, opened two years earlier, focused on local projects. Richard asked Bergevin what he planned to call the division. "The Edelman Global Technology practice," said Bergevin, drawing inspiration from his former employer, which had renamed itself International Business Machines while operating only in the U.S. and a couple places in Canada. "Wow, that's ambitious," said Richard. "If we call ourselves 'global,' that's what we'll become," said Bergevin.

Bergevin and his staff went to work convincing Silicon Valley that Edelman, a Chicago-based agency with a reputation for consumer campaigns, was the ideal P.R. firm to help technology companies take advantage of the worldwide communications revolution. They had success attracting new clients – Ericsson and Adobe, for instance – and expanding the workload for current clients, including Oracle and Data General.

On the Ericsson account, Edelman helped promote the Swedish company's sponsorship of the James Bond movie franchise. In *Tomorrow Never Dies* (1997), James Bond, played by actor Pierce

With its technology practice formally established and headquartered in Silicon Valley, Edelman attracted big names and hot-ticket ventures, including Ericsson and its sponsorship of the James Bond movie franchise.

Brosnan, uses his Ericsson cell phone to blow up safes, drive his Aston Martin, and prevent an evil media mogul from starting World War III. "James Bond Saves the World with Mobile Phone," read the headline of a Reuters newswire story drummed up by Edelman.

The biggest breakthrough for the technology practice came when Edelman won a $3 million-a-year account for PeopleSoft, a business software developer. "The PeopleSoft account put our growth into hyper-speed mode," said Bergevin.

While the most robust Edelman offices had been growing at a healthy 20 to 30 percent annually, the Silicon Valley office doubled its revenues each year. Richard, seeing technology becoming a bigger percentage of total Edelman earnings, looked for other opportunities.

EDELMAN INTERNET SERVICES

In March 1995, with little fanfare and limited goals, Edelman became the first large public relations agency to go online by creating and launching its own website, www.edelman.com.

Edelman invited clients to fax or email news releases to the new Edelman Internet Services division, run by media relations specialist Nancy Ruscheinski in Chicago. Ruscheinski and her small "new media" team would upload the documents onto the Edelman site, where they could be viewed by reporters and consumers around the world.

One of the main reasons Edelman created its own site was simple: It wanted to get into the business of web design.

"I remember feeling so proud because we'd learned HTML and created a home page for ourselves – before anyone else," said Ruscheinski. "But we weren't thinking about revolutionizing communications, we just wanted to help usher our current clients into the Internet era."

With the Edelman website up and running in mid-1995, Ruscheinski headed out to convince clients that they too should have an online presence. Her first stop: Butterball.

"I told them, 'We'd like to build a home page for the Butterball Turkey Talk-Line. The Talk-Line ladies can answer questions online as well as on the phone,'" said Ruscheinski. "I remember the client saying that it didn't make sense, because their customers probably didn't have computers. "But I countered that by saying that it didn't matter if only a few people submitted questions. I told them we'd get credit for evolving the Talk-Line and publicity for trying something new."

Butterball agreed to the project, which did garner plenty of media attention. During Thanksgiving week in 1996, the Turkey Talk-Line website received 550,000 hits. "And that was really the birth of Edelman Interactive Solutions – suddenly, we were in business," said Ruscheinski.

Ruscheinski's group continued to provide website building and Internet marketing services to such clients as Bacardi, Bayer, Visa, and Unilever. Within two years, the division had constructed more than 20 major websites, which accounted for nearly $1 million of the firm's $100 million annual revenue. Edelman hired more technology experts in Chicago, New York, and Silicon Valley, while investing $5 million in software and computer upgrades for the Internet unit. Other public relations firms rushed to keep pace.

GOING INTERACTIVE

Richard pushed to integrate the digital and technology practices into other areas of expertise and throughout the firm's growing network of offices in the U.S. and abroad. He wondered aloud if technology could be the engine to drive Edelman to the top of the field.

"Then, just as the potential of the Internet was becoming a hazy sight on our horizon, Edelman started to work with Microsoft," said Talbot, who at this point was the president of Edelman's U.S. offices. "Our relationship forced us to face, and

Microsoft and Edelman created the ExplorasauraBus, a touring 18-wheeler filled with hands-on displays, to introduce consumers to Microsoft Home computer software products.

then to figure out, a future driven by an entirely different medium that would dramatically change communications."

The tech giant approached Edelman for help getting consumers to overcome their computer fears and embrace products like Microsoft Encarta, a multimedia encyclopedia available through web subscription or CD-ROM. Recognizing a communications shift toward interactivity, Edelman devised a first-of-its-kind, online forum called Encarta on the Record.

Encarta on the Record gathered a series of well-known experts on a given subject, then let Internet users, as well as a live studio audience, ask them questions. Hosted by newswoman Linda Ellerbee, the first Encarta on the Record program examined political divisiveness during the 1996 presidential campaign and featured Senator Bill Bradley, MTV journalist Tabitha Soren, and former Senator Paul Tsongas as panelists. During the Internet broadcast, Microsoft webmasters posted relevant background information from Encarta, even though that information sometimes contradicted what the panelists were saying.

"Encarta on the Record broke new ground for public relations and for Microsoft," said Talbot. "It was a new way of talking to and with audiences. It used the Internet as entertainment. It brought immediacy and relevance to a dry category, and pointed the way to a new form of real-time communication. I don't think any other public relations firm had experimented so boldly with the Internet up to this point. It gave Edelman the ability to reimagine the future and begin to staff for it."

Though a hit with audiences, Encarta on the Record proved to be too expensive to continue. But while Microsoft was forced to pull the plug after only a handful of shows, Encarta on the Record helped the computer giant see the possibilities of combining software, media, and public involvement, and convinced Edelman that the Internet offered far more P.R. applications than it had first imagined.

This included employing the Internet in times of crisis.

IMMEDIATE RESPONSE

In October 1996, Washington State health officials discovered the presence of a deadly strain of E. coli bacteria in unpasteurized apple juice bottled by Odwalla, a West Coast-based natural-foods company. More than 65 people in Washington, California, Colorado, and British Columbia were sickened by the tainted juice, including 14 children and a 16-month-old Colorado girl who subsequently died of kidney failure. Odwalla immediately recalled its products containing apple juice from 4,600 retail outlets in seven western states and Canada.

Odwalla company founders, who had started the natural foods company in Santa Cruz, California, with a motto of "soil to soul, people to planet, and nourishing the body whole," were devastated by the outbreak. Within 24 hours, they called Matthew Harrington, general manager of Edelman San Francisco, and enlisted the firm to help communicate with the media and with customers who may have consumed Odwalla juices.

Edelman immediately set up a media center in the Odwalla offices, which fielded more than 200 calls from reporters the first day. It also established a 1-800 number for consumers, and arranged for Odwalla Chairman Greg Steltenpohl to meet with affected families; "Odwalla Chairman Apologizes as Outbreak Spreads," read a headline in the *Oakland Tribune*.

Matt and his crew also took the unique step of launching a crisis communications website.

Edelman helped juice maker Odwalla recover from an E. coli crisis in 1996. Here, Odwalla chairman Greg Steltenpohl (left) and Edelman's Matthew Harrington pose with new Odwalla products.

Edelman had begun to create and store empty websites (so-called "dark sites") on its servers that could be used in just such an emergency. The Odwalla site, which included questions and answers about the recall and links to government health sites, received roughly 19,000 hits within its first 48 hours of operation.

"The fact that Odwalla's products were distributed throughout the West and at premium prices drew me to the conclusion that its consumers were also likely to be early adopters of the web," said Harrington. "For the crisis, we wanted to let consumers and media know that the company was doing everything possible to communicate. So establishing a web presence was a logical early step. Very shortly the tone of media coverage shifted from recall to showcasing everything this small company was doing to get the facts out via an information-rich website. It was the ultimate proof point." Nevertheless, the outbreak threatened the future of Odwalla, which watched sales plummet by 90 percent, forcing the juice maker to lay off 60 workers. But company executives earned praise for their honest and heartfelt response to the crisis. Odwalla paid hefty fines, donated money to the prevention of food-borne illness, and settled lawsuits with victims. It also took steps to prevent future outbreaks, including a decision to "flash pasteurize" its juices.

A year later, Odwalla introduced a new line of juices and shakes, many without apple juice. The natural foods company also entered the energy bar market, and by the end of 1997 it was again profitable. In 2001, Odwalla was acquired by The Coca-Cola Company for $181 million.

GAME CHANGE

The Odwalla and Encarta campaigns, coupled with the skyrocketing success of the Silicon Valley office, opened many eyes at Edelman. "Suddenly, we saw that information could come from multiple sources simultaneously," said Pam Talbot. "The small voice could compete with the loud one, changing the ladders of influence. Time would be compressed, putting a strain on the facts and a premium on speed. The public's expectations and experiences would be altered in ways we couldn't fully predict. We needed to move fast, and we did."

To Dan, though he stayed away from computers personally, the Internet embraced an approach he had championed since the day he crafted his first public relations scheme for the Toni Company. "We've always emphasized the fact that public relations is a two-way communication," said Dan. "The Internet is a great vehicle for an exchange of ideas. People can ask questions and maintain a dialogue."

Richard, Talbot, and other company executives pushed to integrate websites, interactivity, and high-tech communications into other accounts. They hired more tech experts and loaded new business proposals with new methods of communication. In Chicago, they created a new group – called the Reputation Management group – that would help clients monitor and shape what was being said online about their companies and their products. Renée Edelman got in on the act, conducting media relations for key technology clients.

The company's technology client roster grew around the world. In New York and Chicago, Europe and Asia, Edelman signed up scores of Internet start-ups, software companies, and corporations looking to enter the digital age. The firm's relationship with Microsoft helped Talbot increase the technology business in Seattle and elsewhere in the Northwest. And in Silicon Valley, Edelman signed on to assist the most iconic client of them all.

A JOB FROM JOBS

When Steve Jobs returned to lead Apple in 1997, after a dozen-year separation from the company he cofounded, he fired Apple's P.R. agencies and announced that the company would no longer participate in the big technology trade shows. Jobs wanted to do public relations differently from all other computer companies. So he put out a "casting call" for new P.R. agencies, with the caveat that only agency principals participate in the pitch if their firm made it to the interview stage.

Paul Bergevin and Edelman made the cut, a fact that kept Bergevin up for several nights, worried about how he would approach the brilliant but mercurial Jobs. As soon as Bergevin entered the Apple meeting room for the presentation, Jobs began to pepper him with questions about how to best tell the story of Apple's comeback after several years of failed products and unprofitability.

The Edelman Global Technology practice, led by Paul Bergevin, helped Apple and CEO Steve Jobs conduct an extensive public relations campaign surrounding the 1998 launch of the new iMac desktop computer. The high-profile account boosted Edelman's presence in Silicon Valley and other technology hubs.

future; now it does." The iMac won rave reviews, selling more than a quarter-million units within its first six weeks on the market, making it the most successful computer launch in history at the time. And within a year of Jobs taking over as CEO, Apple went from losing $1 billion annually to profits of more than $300 million for the year. The company never looked back, becoming the world's most valuable corporation by 2012.

Apple. Microsoft. Ericsson. PeopleSoft. Internet services. Reputation management. Crisis communications. Edelman, an agency led by a 76-year-old man who refused to use a computer and his tech-enthusiast son, suddenly found itself at the forefront of the digital communications revolution, ahead of all other large P.R. agencies.

RETURN OF A SON

After five minutes, Jobs leapt to his feet and began to write notes on a whiteboard about the key steps to take in a P.R. campaign. Bergevin realized that the meeting was no longer a pitch. Edelman had been hired.

After Bergevin called Richard to give him the good news, the magnitude of the new work set in. Jobs wanted a team within 30 days. So Bergevin and Richard pulled together tech-savvy people from Edelman offices in Italy, Mexico, and the U.S. to build a 16-person Apple unit. The group was to spend the coming year repositioning the technology company and preparing for the 1998 launch of the new iMac, a computer that, according to industry analysts, would decide the fate of Jobs and Apple.

Working in coordination with a $100 million iMac advertising campaign, Edelman was able to spread the word that Apple and its products were back. In a cover story arranged by Bergevin, *Fortune* magazine declared: "A year and a half ago Apple had no

After a divorce and a series of job offers from Dan, John Edelman had rejoined the firm in 1992 as an account supervisor in Chicago. He enjoyed the client work and the renewed family bond that came from once again working with his father, brother, and sister. Three years after John's return, Dan approached his younger son with an idea.

"My father said, 'John, you are a people person, and everybody is too busy on client work. How would you like to establish a human resources function for us?'" recalled John. "To support the firm's maturation around the world, Edelman needed to become serious about organizing its people practices and systems and operate as one company globally. I jumped at the chance to lead the effort."

According to several independent surveys in the mid-'90s, Edelman scored high in categories such as creativity and campaign effectiveness, but its ratings dipped when it came to client service, administrative management, and

Richard, Roz, and their three daughters (from left to right), baby Amanda, Tory, and Margot ham it up for an Edelman family holiday card.

returned to New York full-time. The European offices, which had been billing $16 million a year and operating in the red before Richard took over, now were profitable and bringing in $20 million annually.

"That experience was invaluable," said Richard. "I learned how to run a multinational business. I learned about NGOs [nongovernmental organizations] for the first time. I learned about multi-country programs, and how you have to flex them to make them work. And I made countless European friends – people we still work with."

For Dan Edelman, Richard's stint managing Edelman Europe along with his son's efforts to build the growing technology and digital practices, confirmed his decision to hand over day-to-day management of the company to Richard. More than ever, Dan wanted to make Edelman the most successful and respected public relations agency in the world. But at the age of 76, he knew that if Edelman was ever to reach the top, Richard would need to lead the way.

At an Edelman general managers meeting at the tony Casino Club in Chicago in September 1997, Dan announced his decision to name Richard the sole CEO of Edelman Public Relations Worldwide. He asked his son to say a few words to the 60 Edelman executives in the room.

As Richard approached the dais, he knew the speech would be a tough one. Hearing his father's announcement brought back a lifetime of images, memories of the large media and client parties at the Edelman home hosted by his parents, of the tough decision to join the firm after business school, of the countless times he had assured his father that he, Richard, knew what he was doing.

employee training. One internal survey found that Edelman employees were spending nearly a third of their time on administrative matters instead of client service.

John created a small human resources team to implement a series of actions that would enhance Edelman's internal administration and help all the offices operate in a more uniform manner. He also oversaw the implementation of a computer system that streamlined the management and reporting of employee information globally, including employee history, training, and performance reviews. They also centralized recruitment, taking the function away from outside recruiters and bringing it in-house.

FORGING NEW LEADERSHIP

In 1996, after Roz gave birth to the couple's third daughter, Amanda, Richard wrapped up his European management responsibilities and

But instead of launching into a revenue forecast or organizational review, Richard pulled a folded piece of paper from his jacket and started to read

In September 1997, Dan appointed his son Richard, to become the sole CEO of the firm.

the poem "The Village Blacksmith" by Henry-Wadsworth Longfellow.

> Under a spreading chestnut tree
> The village smithy stands;
> The smith, a mighty man is he,
> With large and sinewy hands;
> And the muscles of his brawny arms
> Are strong as iron bands.
>
> His hair is crisp, and black, and long,
> His face is like the tan;
> His brow is wet with honest sweat,
> He earns whate'er he can,
> And looks the whole world in the face,
> For he owes not any man.
>
> Week in, week out, from morn till night,
> You can hear his bellows blow;
> You can hear him swing his heavy sledge
> With measured beat and slow,
> Like a sexton ringing the village bell,
> When the evening sun is low.

He stopped reading, and started to cry.

AN ACE OF A DECISION

In 1997, as workers were finishing construction on the new U.S. Open tennis stadium in Queens, New York, city leaders and the country's top tennis officials faced a tough decision: What should they call it?

It needed the right name, yet city representatives and the U.S. Tennis Association couldn't agree on an approach.

Some people argued for a corporate sponsorship to bring in needed revenue. Others pushed for the stadium to be named after former mayor David Dinkins, an avid tennis player who spearheaded the project while in office. A meeting was scheduled to come to an agreement.

Alan G. Schwartz, a USTA board member and tennis partner of Dan's in Chicago, asked Dan to attend. Edelman represented the USTA and Schwartz thought Dan's counsel would be helpful. Throughout the meeting, Dan sat listening to the various suggestions, writing notes with his trademark Flair pen. Then he spoke.

There was only one name they should consider, he advised: Arthur Ashe Stadium.

Ashe, a former U.S. Open champion and lifetime civil rights advocate, had died in 1993 of complications related to AIDS. Ashe's feats on and off the tennis court made him the logical choice. The group agreed, and Arthur Ashe Stadium was christened.

"Dan had this wonderful way of cutting to the chase and helping clients like the USTA do the right thing," said longtime Edelman New York employee Jody Quinn.

"Ashe's Name on Stadium Is an Ace," proclaimed the headline to Dave Anderson's column in *The New York Times* after the decision was announced.

CHAPTER II

NEW LEADERSHIP, NEW CHALLENGES

As Richard settled into the role of CEO, Edelman began to experience several years of steady growth. Fueled by a robust global economy, Edelman strengthened its worldwide presence, opening offices in São Paolo, Buenos Aires, and Taipei (1997); Barcelona and Miami (1998); and Seattle (1999).

Around the world, Edelman helped clients make headlines and increase profits. Edelman China organized fashion shows and hair styling classes on behalf of Vidal Sassoon (Procter & Gamble), a groundbreaking effort that established the line of hair care products as a leading brand and trendsetter in the Asian nation. The new Edelman offices in Korea, which had opened in 1966, and Taiwan helped the agency grow its business elsewhere in Asia, with successful programs for Samsung, UPS, Budweiser, and many other companies.

In Europe, despite a series of management shake-ups, Edelman offices strengthened their capabilities, staging successful campaigns for such clients as Heineken and Bayer.

Edelman offices in the U.S. turned in record profits, with a client roster that included Hershey's, Disney, Nike, and Toys"R"Us. The Edelman Consumer division began to assist coffee giant Starbucks with store launches and promotions.

The mid- to late '90s were a time of steady growth and overseas expansion for Edelman, with many Fortune 500 companies fueling the firm's client roster. Accounts included: Vidal Sassoon, whose eponymous line of hair products is owned by Procter & Gamble; Pão de Açúcar, Brazil's largest supermarket chain; Samsung Electronics, whose vice chairman and CEO Jong Yong Yun is seen here; and UPS.

The Public Affairs practice provided support to Microsoft and its chairman, Bill Gates, as the software giant successfully fought off antitrust lawsuits brought by the federal government and 20 state attorneys general; the Edelman Travel and Hospitality group helped Microsoft launch Expedia, the world's first large-scale, online travel booking service.

The new offices in Buenos Aires, São Paolo, and Miami, coupled with Edelman's office in Mexico City, strengthened the agency's ability to stage public relations campaigns for the Latin-American market. Edelman coordinated Brazil's first nationwide corporate citizenship campaign on behalf of that country's largest supermarket chain, Pão de Açúcar, an effort that promoted Brazilian culture, community enhancement, environmentalism, and health through concerts, recycling initiatives, and school and sporting events.

Here, Dan teaches an Edelman University class to Edelman staffers in a classroom of the Kellogg School of Management at Northwestern University.

Near the end of the millennium, Edelman annual revenues topped the $200 million mark for the first time. A sense of confidence spread through the company's ranks.

GETTING RESOURCEFUL

As revenues and self-assurance grew, so too did the Edelman payroll; in 1998, the firm had 1,800 employees – a 73 percent increase in head count in just two years. The firm's size, expanding global network, and growing diversity led to a series of new human resources initiatives.

Richard decided to boost training at the firm, requiring every worker to accrue a minimum of 24 hours of specialty instruction each fiscal year. In New York, Janice Rotchstein and Jody Quinn had recently instituted a professional skills development program called Edelman University or Edel-U. Its curriculum – which included guest speakers, online courses, and the European Edelman Leadership Academy – was expanded to all Edelman offices in 1998.

In a move aimed at retaining employees in the U.S., the company piloted something called Edelman Escape, an initiative that offered workers $1,000 and an extra week of vacation to pursue a personal dream. Staffers used this opportunity to do things like volunteer as a counselor at a camp for children with cancer, assist a Bolivian charity with sustainability projects, and surprise a young son with a trip to Washington, D.C., to learn about the U.S. Constitution.

At the same time, Richard and other company leaders recognized that the firm needed to do more to define itself and its mission. Internal surveys revealed that most Edelman staffers felt good about the general direction of the firm, yet only a third felt that they were well informed about the company's goals.

So Edelman launched a plan called Working for a Shared Focused Future, the aim of which was to globalize its vision mission values (VMV) statement. Led by Pam Talbot and Michael Morley, and managed by Janice Rotchstein and John Edelman, VMV gathered input from more than 800 employees at all levels. As a result of the exercise, the new Edelman mission would be: "To provide public relations counsel and strategic communications services that enable our clients to build strong relationships and to influence attitudes and behaviors in a complex world."

More important, VMV defined the Edelman personality, using the words "quality," "integrity," "respect," "entrepreneurial spirit," and "mutual benefits" – many of the same words that were often used to describe Dan.

STUBBING OUT CIGARETTES

The VMV process signaled a change in the Edelman culture. It pushed the company to be a truly global firm, not just an American P.R. agency with offices abroad. It also forced employees to reexamine their business practices. For Richard, that meant addressing an issue that had gnawed at him since childhood. "I called my dad and told him we were going to stop all tobacco work," said Richard. "I'd had enough."

While it had never been the primary, agency of record for any of the big tobacco companies, Edelman had handled tobacco-funded campaigns for more than three decades. Toronto, Montreal, and London were among the offices most affected by Richard's decision. Edelman Canada had promoted the du Maurier Classic, an LPGA tournament sponsored by Imperial Tobacco. And Edelman London represented the Tobacco

Advisory Council, the industry lobbying group in Great Britain.

Richard's actions cost Edelman a few million dollars in billings, but quickly paid big dividends in increased health care business and company morale. More and more,

In the late 1990s, Richard ended all tobacco-related work.

health care companies and government agencies were refusing to allow P.R. firms and advertising companies to even bid on campaigns if they represented tobacco.

In later years, Richard took his antismoking efforts a step further, offering to pay employees $2,000 if they would quit smoking. Dozens have taken him up on the proposal.

EDELMAN WELCOMES A SISTER

In 1998, the company launched PR21, a second P.R. brand and sister agency to handle projects and clients that would present a conflict-of-interest situation to Edelman Public Relations Worldwide. Co-headquartered in New York and Chicago, the new agency specialized in the technology, new media, consumer, and health care fields. Within two years it had signed on more than 70 clients, including such Fortune 500 companies as 3M, Whirlpool, and Motorola.

"It was a new firm for the 21st-century economy," said Renée Edelman who joined PR21 as its new-media manager. "PR21 had a very creative, entrepreneurial spirit. Just like my father. We had a lot of quick success with several Internet companies such as GeoCities."

The following year, Edelman created StrategyOne, a market research organization and another firm under the Daniel J. Edelman Inc. holding company. It also purchased a small design company – later called Blue – to handle issue and advocacy advertising, an increasingly frequent Edelman client need.

TIME FOR LOVE

After nearly 50 years together, Dan and Ruth had more time to spend with each other now that Richard was in charge of the firm. "Our love grew stronger once Dan turned the firm over to Richard," said Ruth. "Dan didn't have to hustle as much. He didn't have all the pressure. We had time for ourselves. We held hands and kissed more than we ever had before."

In honor of Ruth's 70th birthday, in 1999, Dan hosted a party for 100 friends in the ballroom of the venerable Casino Club in Chicago. Attendees included family members and people whose lives Ruth had touched over the years, among them Senator Charles Percy, Michael Deaver, and long-time friend Margie Benton, who hailed Ruth as the Chicago Gold Coast's "hostess with the mostess."

With a flute of champagne in his hand, Dan praised his wife for her selfless work on behalf of firm and family. He extolled her intuition, her kind heart, and her ability to give people a needed boost or a second chance – qualities, he said, that benefited Dan himself, their children, and the company.

Dan and Ruth continued their charity efforts, contributing dollars and time to organizations such as the Lyric Opera of Chicago, the Save the Children Federation, the Chicago Project for Violence Prevention, and the Committee for Economic Growth of Israel. They also visited Edelman offices around the world, serving as "goodwill ambassadors."

Though Dan refused to rest on his laurels, continuing to work out of the Chicago office every day, peers began to celebrate his contribution to the field of public relations. The awards started to pile up, including a Golden Anvil from the Public Relations Society of America, its top award, and induction into the Arthur Page Society Hall of Fame, the highest honor given by the organization of corporate communications executives. In 1999, he

Ruth and Dan at Ruth's 70th birthday party at Chicago's Casino Club. After Richard assumed the role of CEO, Ruth and Dan enjoyed having more time together, which included traveling around the world to visit Edelman offices.

received the first-ever Outstanding Achievement Award from the China International Public Relations Association for "bringing modern public relations practices to China."

A RUDE AWAKENING

From his office overlooking Times Square, Richard went about the business of leading Edelman. Though he worked just as hard as his father ever had, rising each morning before dawn to dash off emails or make phone calls to managers around the world, Richard's first several years as CEO had come easy. Perhaps too easy. A serious problem with Edelman's computer billing and expense system would be the first in a series of setbacks to shake Richard and the firm.

As the company became increasingly global and diverse in its operations, Richard had recruited a new chief financial officer who made the decision that Edelman's spreadsheets and manually produced bills needed to be replaced with modern financial reporting software. Richard and the CFO tapped PeopleSoft, a client, to install a new system, which was up and running within a few months.

The system seemed to be working well, until the day it started generating bogus bills for Edelman clients. Next, it wouldn't allow employees to process their expenses. The computer glitches were growing at leaps and bounds and into a full-blown crisis. Frantic efforts by the CFO and a team of technicians did little to ease the emergency. Unable to bill clients, Edelman ran up its line of credit from zero to $20 million in four months. "There's nothing like a near-death experience to prepare you for running a company," said Richard. "It was a fiasco that could have ruined us."

Richard went into emergency mode, firing the CFO, enlisting the efforts of professional services giant Deloitte, and calling top clients individually to let them each know what was happening.

After a year, Edelman had corrected the system and paid back its creditors. "My father was a pretty good sport about it," said Richard. "I just thank God it happened during an 'up' economy."

LOSING INDEPENDENCE?

Richard was learning that the role of CEO required a certain amount of skepticism. He vowed to ask more questions and test future systems before installing them. He also made a mental note not to be surprised by anything, a declaration that was tested only a few months later.

In May 1999, Edelman employees were shocked to read a handful of news articles covering an address Dan had recently made to the Public Relations Society of America's Counselor's Academy during which he had discussed the subject of selling Edelman. "I'm not sure we'll do it now, but it's possible," said Dan, as quoted in *PR Week*. "We might sell part of our shares to an ad agency. We might go public with part of our shares."

The sale of Fleishman-Hillard to the Omnicom Group two years earlier had left Edelman as the only independent public relations firm among the top 10. "If I didn't have Richard as a successor there is no question what I would have done," Dan told the "Inside PR" newsletter.

While Dan's comments surprised Richard, he tried to calm the situation by telling employees and reporters that he and his father had been approached by numerous advertising agencies and conglomerates over the years, but that they had no intention of selling.

A JARRING SURVEY

Edelman leadership received another eye-opener when they learned the results of the 2000 Harris/Impulse P.R. Client Survey, the industry's most respected assessment of P.R. agency capabilities.

Edelman, which had always received strong grades from the survey, suddenly got failing marks in categories such as quality control, attention to detail, and responsiveness. Worse, the agency suffered big declines in two of its historic strengths, the creativity and quality of writing categories. Follow-up internal surveys and the loss of several longtime clients seemed to confirm the Harris findings.

Shaken, Richard and his managers, taking note of the shortcomings revealed by the surveys, debated the best way to go about addressing them. "The report basically said that we were an agency that had many P.R. stars, but that we too often missed things when it came to the basics," said Richard. "It was a huge wake-up call. We knew we needed to change our way of doing business."

THE DOT.COMEDOWN

Despite the growing sense of dissatisfaction revealed by the Harris Survey, Edelman's revenues continued to reach record levels, the result of a growing workload fueled by dot.com start-ups and new business with multinational clients. Edelman and PR21 signed up new clients at a frenzied rate – sometimes without having time to conduct due diligence. "About half my time was spent on new business," said Renée in a *New York Times* article. "Anyone who'd call, we'd rush out to see."

The boom forced Edelman to staff offices with Internet communications experts as quickly as it could. "It was a wild and fun place," said Ellen Edelman, a technology specialist, not related to Dan's family, who worked in the firm's New York tech practice at that time. "There was this anything-goes mentality, an entrepreneurial spirit to the extreme."

In New York, the technology practice ballooned to 66 people to service such accounts as EDS (Electronic Data Systems), Fuji, and telecommunications company Global Crossing, as well as dozens of smaller Internet start-ups. The firm experienced similar rates of growth in its Chicago and Texas offices as well as in a small new branch in Boston.

Patrick McGuire, who sold his Seattle-based P.R. agency to Edelman in 1999 and stayed on as general manager, remembers executives from dot.com start-ups walking through Edelman's doors and promising large stock options and wild payoffs. "P.R. firms were the glitterati of the new information age," he said. "They were getting huge amounts of money to send out often empty press releases."

McGuire also remembers Richard and Dan rejecting all equity offers, telling office managers that that would constitute a potential conflict of interest. They stressed that Edelman was a professional services firm, not a shareholder. That stance, though correct, made it harder for McGuire and other managers to retain some employees, who fled to dot.com companies or P.R. agencies that accepted equity payments.

In the aftermath of the dot.com bust, Edelman fared better than many other P.R. firms, thanks to its independence and debt-free status.

Signs of a slowdown in the dot.com economy came slowly at first – a small number of unpaid bills, a couple of clients declaring bankruptcy – but by the end of 2001, the dot.com sector was in an out-and-out free fall. "Edelman had gone from just under $100 million in annual revenues in 1996 to $220 million in 2001," said Richard. "In 2002, we were running the company as if we were heading for $240 million, then all of a sudden it went back down to $200-220 million. It was just, bang."

Public relations agencies were forced to take drastic action. Many eliminated their tech divisions. Others folded altogether.

At Edelman, the necessary corrective action was severe but not ruinous. The Boston office was closed, the tech divisions in Texas and Chicago were downsized, and the New York tech practice was slashed from 66 people to fewer than 10. But Richard refused to eliminate the practice altogether. He did everything possible to retain company talent in order to be ready when the economy improved.

"Were we geniuses?" said Richard. "No. We had one year where we had $3 million in unpaid bills. But the dot.com bust was one of those times when being independent and having no debt really paid off. We were able to accept a few years of slow growth and wait for the economy to come around."

THE DAY THE WORLD CHANGED

The second Tuesday of September 2001 had been scheduled to be a busy day for the Edelman New York office. The firm had organized several large public events, including a live hotline for people interested in learning more about ADHD (attention-deficit/hyperactivity disorder) and a promotional event in Times Square for Planter's Nuts, featuring Mr. Peanut.

But hectic schedules were no problem for the office. Pam Talbot had promoted Matthew Harrington, the former general manager of Edelman San Francisco/West Coast, as head of the agency's biggest office. Harrington's calm demeanor and thoughtful encouragement gave the New York staff members a feeling they could accomplish anything.

Shortly before 9:00 o'clock that morning, Harrington heard news reports of a plane crash at the World Trade Center. Then he received a phone call from Therese Caruso, the Edelman executive overseeing the Planter's event. She wanted to know what was causing all the media to cancel her bookings so quickly. "I was still trying to figure out what was going on, so I didn't know what to tell her," said Harrington. "Then I looked out my window and saw the second plane hit the South Tower."

In a scene tragically repeated around the world, Edelman staffers in New York were frozen in disbelief after hijackers had flown two commercial airliners into the Twin Towers of the World Trade Center eventually causing the buildings to collapse and resulting in the death of nearly 3,000 people. For Harrington the tragedy hit on many levels.

Harrington's brother Frank worked at Marsh & McLennan, the large professional services company with offices in the North Tower. After leaving several panicked phone messages for Frank, Harrington asked a young staffer to wait in the ground floor lobby on the off chance his brother showed up. Just as word trickled in that American Airlines Flight 11 had directly hit the Marsh & McLennan offices on floors 93-100, Frank appeared at Edelman. After an early arrival at work that morning he had stepped out to see a friend who was running in a New York City primary race being held that day. More than 350 Marsh & McLennan employees and contractors – everyone who was present in the office – died when the plane slammed into the building.

In the wake of 9/11, makeshift memorials went up all over the New York metropolitan area. Edelman helped to set up and staff a bereavement center for Cantor Fitzgerald, which lost more than 650 employees in the attacks, including Suria Clarke, who had just left Edelman to work for the bond-trading firm.

"I also knew that Cantor Fitzgerald, one of our clients, had its offices in the North Tower," Harrington said. "In fact, I'd had lunch a month before with Fred Varacchi, the president of their eSpeed division. He had asked me if it was okay to hire away Suria Clarke, one of our employees. Not wanting to stand in her way I said, 'okay.'"

Clarke and 657 other Cantor Fitzgerald employees died in the attack. The bond-trading firm had been cofounded in 1947 by B. Gerald Cantor, a classmate of Dan's at DeWitt Clinton High School. It would suffer more losses than any other single company.

Fighting an upheaval of emotions, Harrington closed the New York office, giving staffers the opportunity to try to get in touch with loved ones. He gathered senior management at the nearby Harvard Club and frantically attempted to account for all his employees.

A bit later that morning, Richard Edelman landed at the airport in Omaha, Nebraska, planning to attend a golf and tennis outing for CEOs hosted by business magnate Warren Buffet. Watching the unfolding story of the horrific events on an airport television screen he learned that more than 70 of his wife Roz's former colleagues at Keefe, Bruyette & Woods – an investment firm that had occupied three floors of the South

Tower – had died when the building collapsed. Roz had left the firm in 1996 after the birth of the couple's third daughter, Amanda.

A PLACE TO GRIEVE

As Harrington made certain that everyone on his staff was alive and safe, he reached out to Cantor Fitzgerald and other clients, reopening the Edelman office in the afternoon of 9/11 for their use. A dozen Cantor employees who had escaped the attacks set up an impromptu office at Edelman. Meanwhile, Edelman employees, led by Holli Rafkin-Sax, then head of the firm's financial communications practice, helped Cantor CEO Howard Lutnick field hundreds of media calls.

In the days that followed, Edelman coordinated a Cantor Fitzgerald bereavement center in the Pierre Hotel in Manhattan, a place where family members of deceased or missing Cantor employees could gather to seek support and consolation in one another. More than 100 Edelman employees volunteered to staff the center, which Edelman operated without charge. "Everybody chipped in to help clients in the hours and days after 9/11," said Richard. "It was one of my proudest moments."

Like other workers in New York, Edelman employees returned to their jobs with heavy hearts and a desire to contribute to the healing process in some way. Harrington brought in grief counselors and allowed people to work from home if they wished.

Dan had watched the tragedy unfold from his office in Chicago. Calling the events of 9/11 "expressions of hate," the former Army public information officer dictated a memo to staff that cited American resilience during its wars and times of great challenge. "We will never submit to these futile efforts to handicap or even

destroy our way of life. To the contrary, these despicable actions will serve to reenergize us, pull us together and enable us to re-commit to helping build an even better society."

AIDING THE AID GIVERS

In Washington, D.C., where 9/11 terrorists had flown a hijacked plane into the Pentagon, killing 184 men and women, Edelman staffers opened their homes to clients from out of town who were stranded when the federal government shut down all non-military flights. And in the days that followed, when one of its clients found itself in a full-blown 9/11 scandal, Edelman was there to provide assistance.

Responding to the attacks, Americans across the country had rushed to give blood, contribute money, or help in any way they could. The American Red Cross, the country's oldest and most respected relief organization, was the obvious charity of choice for many people. Donators

In September 2001, Matthew Harrington, a specialist in corporate positioning and reputation management, was the general manager of the New York office.

Mike Deaver approached former Senate Majority Leader George Mitchell (pictured here) to broker a solution for the Red Cross when the charity found itself at the center of a controversy over its use of 9/11 donations.

president of the Edelman D.C. office. "His involvement helped convince people the Red Cross was serious about a course correction and was taking the right path forward."

At the urging of Mitchell and Edelman, the Red Cross announced that all $543 million raised in its Liberty Fund would be paid to 9/11 victims and families.

With the controversy behind it, the charity went back to work preparing for future emergencies. "Within weeks of the announcement, research showed public confidence in the Red Cross had been restored to the very high levels it enjoyed prior to the crisis," said Rehg.

contributed $543 million to the Red Cross Liberty Disaster Fund to aid 9/11 victims and their families.

Within weeks, the initial surge of support would turn into a heated debate about the Red Cross's plans to use some of the donations for purposes not related to 9/11. The charity also came under fire for collecting more blood than was actually needed. Red Cross president Dr. Bernadine Healy was forced to resign her post on October 26.

The Red Cross, worried that the scandal would threaten not just its 9/11 campaign but future relief efforts, enlisted Michael Deaver and the Edelman team in Washington, D.C., for help. Deaver immediately realized what was needed – a senior statesman who could broker a solution. He also knew the right man for the job – former Senate Majority Leader George Mitchell.

"Bringing in George Mitchell was key to solving the crisis because he was so credible with every constituency," said Rob Rehg, the current

THINKING OUTSIDE THE BOX

The day after the attacks, Richard and Pam Talbot issued a memo to all staff that outlined their views on how Edelman employees should proceed with their P.R. work in the short term. They counseled workers to "focus on internal audiences first," "extend help to the community," and avoid "activities that are opportunistic and exploitative." They went on to urge staffers to "reconsider spokespeople for P.R. programs, as real experts are preferred over celebrities," and refrain from using "the media preoccupation [with 9/11] as an opportunity to release and 'hide' [a client's] bad news."

One issue Edelman and other P.R. firms faced in the aftermath of 9/11 was how to carry on with product launches and other campaigns that had been in the planning stages for months. Account leaders agonized over these decisions, not wanting to do anything that would be considered insensitive, yet not wanting to allow actions by terrorists to dampen Americans' spirit and resolve.

In one such example, Pam Talbot and a team of Edelman associates had been preparing a large-scale campaign to promote the release of Microsoft's first foray into the gaming device market, the Xbox. This was a market that had up to then been dominated by Nintendo and the Sony PlayStation. Instead of targeting stores, Edelman and Microsoft were planning to focus directly on consumers. To build buzz within the gaming community, Edelman had sent Xbox consoles to high-profile video gamers, bloggers, and to "to the teenaged kids of tech editors rather than to the editors themselves," said Talbot.

For the day of the launch, November 15, 2001, Edelman had planned to host 24-hour gaming marathons on both coasts that would allow "thousands of gaming enthusiasts to get their hands on the product and to demonstrate both its power and its stability to their cohorts," said Talbot. As a capper event, Edelman had arranged for Xbox to go on sale minutes after midnight at the new flagship Toys"R"Us store in Times Square, where Microsoft Chairman Bill Gates himself would be on hand to play Xbox games with the first customers in line. The events of September 11 put everything on hold.

But as activity in New York began to return to normal, Mayor Rudolf Giuliani and other community leaders encouraged visitors to return.

When Edelman asked the mayor for his thoughts about the Xbox event, he urged them to carry on with the plans.

On the night of the launch, enthusiastic video gamers turned out in droves, lining up around the block to be the first buyers. Microsoft sold more than one million of its game consoles in North America in the following three weeks, making Xbox the quickest selling gaming device in history up to that time.

Equally important, the Edelman campaign helped bring a few heartening smiles to a city that badly needed some.

When it was launched in November 2001, Xbox became the quickest selling gaming device in history. Eager for visitors to return to New York, the Giuliani administration encouraged Edelman and Microsoft to carry on with their plans for an Xbox launch extravaganza in Times Square.

TOWARD A GREATER GOOD

The comments Richard made about the importance of community in the days and months after 9/11 struck a chord with the firm's employees, who, in the tragedy's wake, longed for deeper, more meaningful assignments that would contribute to a greater good rather than just a company's bottom line.

In memos and emails, Richard expanded on his views. Corporate messages should focus on their relevance to society as a whole, not simply to the commercial world, he counseled. Edelman clients should "commit to accountability and responsibility." "Employees and customers want business processes that are sustainable and reflect the highest ethical standard. Your philosophy should be clear; this is a time when living corporate values is paramount."

His words, which were meant to address the aftermath of 9/11, now were being construed by company employees as having much broader

"The Lower Manhattan website was more than just another account," said Edelman's Russell Dubner. "It was an opportunity to do something for a city we love." This page was one of hundreds that Edelman would create to keep the public apprised of the recovery and rebuilding efforts in Lower Manhattan.

meaning. Taking a cue from their boss, Edelman staffers and executives around the world gradually shifted the focus of many existing campaigns while seeking others that embodied greater humanitarianism.

"A lot of people at Edelman were searching for a sense of purpose after 9/11," said Russell Dubner, who had joined Edelman straight out of college in 1992 and by 2001 had risen to the rank of executive vice president of the New York office's Corporate and Public Affairs group. "They wanted to know how they could best contribute."

When Dubner received a request for proposal from the New York City mayor's office to create a comprehensive website that would detail relevant news and information about the recovery and rebuilding efforts in Lower Manhattan, he knew the company had to bid on the project. Eighty other

Like many businesses located in New York City, Edelman aided 9/11 recovery efforts through volunteerism, donations, and projects that helped rebuild the city.

P.R. firms had the same idea, but Edelman won the account.

The problem was that Edelman didn't receive its marching orders until July 2002, and new mayor Michael Bloomberg wanted the site up and running before the first-year anniversary of 9/11. Edelman employees assigned to the project were to be tested as never before.

Edelman writers and web specialists teamed up with the engineering and consulting firm Parsons Brinkerhoff and its senior vice president Janette Sadik-Khan to work nights and weekends to successfully launch the website. The final product – www.lowermanhattan.info – included regularly updated transit schedules, environmental quality reports, rebuilding updates, and entertainment listings, becoming the go-to source of information about Lower Manhattan. Dubner and his team then implemented a media relations, advertising, and community outreach effort to boost awareness of the website.

"The Lower Manhattan website was more than just another account," said Dubner. "It was an opportunity to do something for a city we love." The project not only "showed Edelman at its best," according to Dubner, it strengthened office camaraderie and furthered Richard's push for work that enhanced communities. Many such opportunities would lie ahead.

In 2005, Edelman continued its P.R. efforts on behalf of Lower Manhattan with a communications campaign called "This is 2010 . . . It's Happening Now."

STANDING UP FOR DIVERSITY

In the late 1990s, Edelman's Seattle office represented gay.com, a social networking site for the gay community that was, at the time, a little start-up making its way during the boom years of the dot.com industry. At the same time, the New York office was representing a global Christian humanitarian organization, an account that paid Edelman five times more than the small gay.com account.

The humanitarian organization "got wind that we were representing gay.com and asked that we resign the business," recalled Patrick McGuire, then head of the Seattle office. "They told our New York office that if we didn't do so, they would pull their business."

McGuire and Nancy Turett, whose health care department was in charge of the humanitarian organization, brought the situation to (U.S. CEO) Pam Talbot's attention, not quite sure what the outcome would be. "We were talking about a lot of money," said McGuire.

McGuire remembers Talbot's exact words as if she had spoken them today: "Well, we would never do that. That's against our values."

"She'd talked to Richard about it as well," said McGuire. "I remember thinking how courageous it was of Edelman to do that, and what that said to me as a civil rights advocate."

According to McGuire, "A day after the humanitarian organization heard the message that, no, Edelman would not resign gay.com's business, it came back to the firm and said, 'You know, you are right. You really made us think. You can represent whomever you want.'"

CHAPTER 12

BETTING ON THE FUTURE

As Edelman neared its 50th anniversary in October 2002, Dan sat down to dictate a memo to all staff members in which he reflected on the firm that bore his name. He wrote: "It is my proud legacy to know that we've played a key role in establishing the standards of public relations and that we have made particular contributions in terms of establishing an ethical code of practice and pioneering in so many different areas."

Looking back over the firm's history, Dan cited his own efforts to develop consumer marketing public relations as well as the firm's expansion into Europe and Asia; he then singled out Richard, U.S. CEO Pam Talbot, and others for their work in creating new practices at Edelman, including health care communications, financial P.R., public affairs, and crisis communications. "You inspire me with your devotion to your work," he concluded.

Dan encouraged employees not to be discouraged by the economic downturn then affecting the U.S. and much of the world. "It's going to be a rough ride for a while, but there's a bright future ahead. I look forward to sharing it with you."

Edelman, like all other large P.R. firms, was still suffering from the effects of 9/11, on top of a series of corporate scandals involving companies like Enron, Tyco, and Global Crossing (an Edelman client), as well as the recession. Yet Edelman was faring better than most of its competitors, especially the ones owned

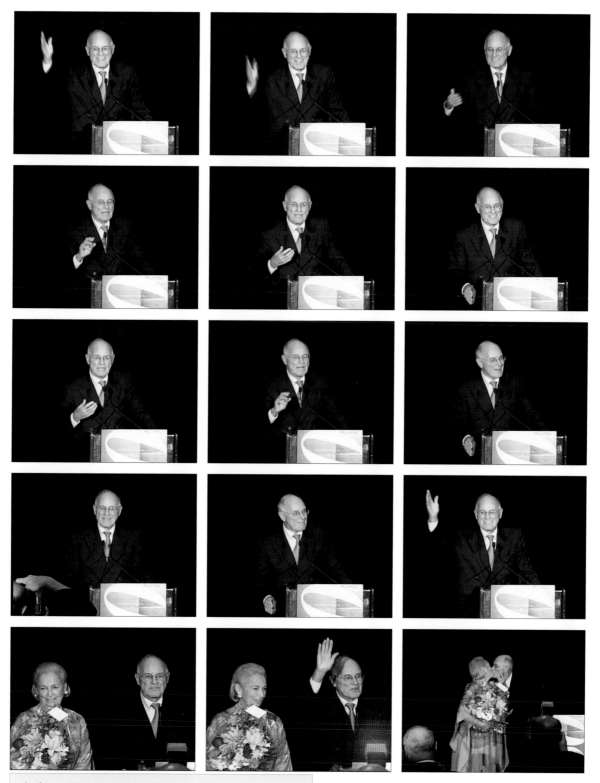

The firm celebrated its 50th anniversary with a dinner at the New York Botanical Garden. Dan is pictured here addressing the evening's guests, which included staff, clients, and friends. Ruth joins Dan on stage to pay tribute to his achievements.

by advertising holding companies. The economic downturn had forced many publicly held firms to eliminate practices and make drastic cuts in staff in order to meet shareholder demands. Having flirted off and on with the idea of selling the firm, Dan was happy once again to have kept Edelman independent. Being privately held again proved to be an advantage.

With Ruth by his side, Dan continued to visit Edelman offices around the world, chatting up employees about their work and prodding general managers always to strive to do better. He also continued to send out his famous (and sometimes infamous) Dan-o-Grams to staff; missives that praised their efforts or conveyed blunt critiques. "You have to write in a genuine way," he once wrote to an employee. "This is too much B.S. Thanks, Dan."

THE RELATIONSHIP IMPERATIVE

While Dan saw the Edelman 50th anniversary as a time of reflection, Richard used it as a launch-ing pad. The recession, the corporate scandals, and 9/11 had changed his views about the overall role of public relations. He decided Edelman needed to change. The entire industry needed to change.

Over the next couple of years, Richard would unveil a series of measures that would dramatically alter the way Edelman operated, changes that had the potential to set the company back significantly should they fail. He began with a vision that challenged corporations – and the P.R. firms that worked for them – to rethink the fundamental way they communicated with the world.

In a paper called "The Relationship Imperative" that appeared in the *Journal of Integrated Communications* published by Northwestern University's Medill School of Journalism, Richard declared the traditional model of top-down corporate communications in which people received one-way information from advertising and large media outlets was dead.

Citing the growth of the Internet, the explosion in the number of news and information sources, the increasing demand for corporate accountability and citizenship, and the rise in the influence of nongovernmental organizations, Richard prescribed a new way for businesses to engage customers.

"The future of business is not about selling, but about building relationships," he wrote. He urged businesses to identify their core constituencies, then connect with them through a wide variety of channels that allow for two-way communication. He encouraged companies to craft "master narratives" that would articulate corporate ideals and urged them to become definitive sources of credible information by engaging directly with their audiences. In this new era, he said, companies needed to be transparent and socially responsible.

In 2002, as the firm celebrated its 50th anniversary, Richard articulated his vision for a new model of communication. Companies, he argued, must connect with their constituencies through a wide variety of channels that allow for two-way communication.

"There has been a seismic shift in the market-place," he continued. "Today, the world of business is everyone's business. Companies cannot afford to withdraw from engaging multiple audiences. Meaningful engagement with stakeholders will be a true source of competitive advantage to those companies willing to forge this new path."

Acting on those words, Edelman announced the results of a rebranding effort, led by global public affairs head Leslie Dach and health care chief Nancy Turett, that changed the firm's name from Edelman Public Relations Worldwide to simply Edelman. The new name reflected Edelman's widespread recognition as a global P.R. firm, as well as the agency's growing number of internal practices and outside specialty firms, which now included Blue (advertising), First&42nd (management consulting), BioScience Communications (medical education and publishing), and Strategy One (research). In addition, Richard had recently purchased The Headline Group, the No. 1 independent P.R. firm in Atlanta, and folded it into Edelman. Headline Group president Claudia Patton stayed on to lead Edelman operations in Atlanta and the Southeast.

Edelman also now had a new logo that included a brandmark of two overlapping triangles, symbolizing the partnership between firm and client. The brandmark is open to one side, suggesting the more open communications outlined by Richard in his Relationship Imperative. The specialty firms adopted similarly shaped marks with a variety of colors to help differentiate their individual areas of expertise.

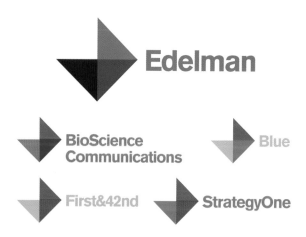

BUILDING TRUST

In the new era of two-way communications, trust and credibility would need to become paramount. No longer could companies and organizations simply issue information and expect the public to accept it without question. This fact hit home with Richard after watching the street protests during the 1999 World Trade Organization meetings, the so-called "Battle of Seattle." These protests are all about trust, he thought.

After watching the protests at the 1999 World Trade Organization meeting in Seattle, Richard created an annual survey on trust called the Edelman Trust Barometer.

The principles of building trust

Trust is the last word of political...

"While American companies abroad can still make use of universal imagery, they should 'go local' whenever possible in how they present themselves."

Sixth Annual Edelman Trust Barometer
A Global Study of Opinion Leaders

Edelman

The Edelman Trust Barometer is now conducted in 25 countries and involves 35,000 respondents. The annual Barometers study trust in four key institutions – government, business, media, and NGOs – as well as communications channels and sources.

In future years, the Trust Barometer surveys grew to encompass 25 countries and 35,000 respondents. Richard began to unveil the results to media and business leaders at a much-sought-after event that coincided with the annual World Economic Forum in Davos, Switzerland.

Richard had long counseled clients to become content providers and storytellers. Now, with the Trust Barometer, Edelman was doing that very thing itself. The surveys also helped connect the Edelman offices around the world and made the firm's work "more science-based," said Richard. "We started to behave more like a professional services firm than a traditional P.R. agency."

ENHANCING QUALITY

While promoting "trust" to the world, Richard was also preaching the importance of "quality" within Edelman. The results of the 2000 Harris/Impulse P.R. Client Survey – which had suggested that Edelman had slipped in quality and client service – still gnawed at him. Some managers blamed the findings on cutbacks the firm had made during the recession, but Richard, Pam Talbot, and other company leaders thought the problem went deeper. They suspected that employees were focusing too much on their own creativity and not enough on clients.

Edelman had made some operational changes following the release of the Harris Survey, but Richard thought the firm needed to do more. From a business perspective, he told his senior

"I talked to Leslie Dach and our research guy and told them that we needed to learn more about trust," said Richard. "How much trust does the public place in governments, NGOs, companies, and the media? Who do they trust as their preferred sources of information?"

The following year, the firm produced a small study called the Edelman Trust Barometer that detailed levels of trust in various institutions in four countries – Germany, France, Great Britain, and the United States. Among other results, the survey found a high level of trust in NGOs and falling levels of trust in well-known CEOs.

Richard decided to make the Edelman Trust Barometer an annual survey and to distribute the results without charge. "People said I was crazy, but I wanted the findings to become part of the common language of communications," said Richard. "I felt that we would all be better off if we knew more about trust."

managers, it would be far easier to grow Edelman through satisfied clients than to spend time and money finding new ones

So in 2002, Richard announced that "quality" would be the company's No. 1 business objective. He then unveiled a comprehensive, half-million-dollar initiative called the Edelman Global Quality Program (or Q Program, for short), which was designed to measure and enhance the company's work product. He tapped Talbot to oversee the effort and named a chief quality officer – Janice Rotchstein, who had worked for John Edelman in human resources. The Q Program was rolled out in several stages.

Rotchstein first sent out online questionnaires to clients around the world asking them to answer questions about Edelman's service. The responses, which were returned to Rotchstein in New York and mid-level and senior managers throughout the firm, allowed Edelman to better understand how its work was being perceived by clients and try to make changes accordingly.

At the same time, Edelman boosted its employee training and support efforts, expanding Edelman University, offering more courses online, creating an intranet site to showcase best practices, pairing staffers with mentors, and initiating rewards for employees who embraced the commitment to quality.

The results were quickly evident. Edelman experienced an increase in its work quality and client service rankings in industry surveys such as the Harris Survey and the Holmes Report. The Q Program was here to stay.

GROWING GLOBAL

With the economy in 2003 starting to improve, several large Edelman clients approached the firm wanting to conduct an increased number of public relations campaigns in different parts of the world.

But while they liked Edelman's worldwide reach, some were wary of having to coordinate with each office individually; they wanted a simpler system.

Up until that point, Edelman had been organized by geography and by practice (technology, consumer, public affairs, etc.). It was now clear that the new global economy called for a new approach, so Pam Talbot created what was called the Edelman Global Client Relationship Management program, or GCRM. Through the GCRM approach, Edelman assigned a senior-level staffer to its largest multinational clients who would serve as the client's single, primary contact, setting the strategy and ensuring continuity and consistency across all campaign efforts.

The approach quickly became a hit. Clients such as Starbucks, AstraZeneca, Microsoft, and Johnson & Johnson now dealt with one senior Edelman manager regardless of the type of project or its location.

Julianna Richter, who was one of the company's first GCRM managers and who currently leads the GCRM program, said the approach has also been a huge benefit to clients in times of emergency. "If there's a crisis anywhere in the world we can have

Julianna Richter is president of the Global Client Relationship Management program.

a fully briefed team on the ground within a day," said Richter. "That's because there is a central repository of knowledge about the client and its business with little time needed for ramp-up."

A WORLD OF CRISES

In early 2003, one such emergency struck in Canada with the outbreak of SARS – severe

The deadly form of pneumonia, which had spread from Hong Kong to 37 countries, ultimately claimed the lives of 44 Toronto residents and forced the quarantine of nearly 20,000 people. No city outside Asia was hit harder than Toronto. Fortunately, two years earlier, Edelman Toronto had updated the health ministry's crisis communications plan and managed a crisis simulation based on a pandemic.

Edelman was instrumental in persuading the World Health Organization to lift an advisory curtailing travel to Toronto following an outbreak of SARS in that city.

acute respiratory syndrome. On March 26, for the first time in Ontario's history, Premier Ernie Eves declared a provincial health emergency, and the province's Ministry of Health and Long-Term Care engaged Edelman Canada, led by Charles Fremes, to provide advice and support.

Then in late April, the World Health Organization issued an advisory urging people to avoid all nonessential travel to Toronto. City leaders were stunned. They felt they had contained the spread of the disease; now they had to deal with severe economic losses caused by a large drop in tourism and canceled conventions. They needed public relations help to attempt to get the advisory lifted and to restore the city's image.

Canadian officials and staffers from the Edelman Toronto, Brussels, and London offices quickly provided WHO leaders in Geneva with all the information they would need to reverse their decision; the advisory was lifted in a matter of days. As the epidemic subsided, Edelman's role evolved to help Toronto with a campaign to spread the word that the city was again safe to visit.

In the aftermath of the tsunami that hit Southeast Asia in 2004, Edelman donated more than $150,000 in services to Save the Children, a relief organization.

A far more deadly disaster struck Asia in 2004 – a 9.0 earthquake under the Indian

Edelman helped Save the Children produce reports that included children's stories of survival. The materials helped raise more than $250 million following the 2004 Southeast Asian tsunami.

and online reports – titled "Through the Eyes of the Children" – that detailed relief activities while sharing personal stories of children affected by the disaster. "[The reports] will allow our hundreds of thousands of donors to know that the commitment they made, that the trust they put in Save the Children has resulted in brighter futures for children and families," said Charles MacCormack, president of the charitable organization at the time.

With its credibility reinforced, Save the Children went on to raise more than $250 million to provide water, food, shelter, and health care to residents in impacted areas, as well as to find thousands of homes for orphans.

DOG FOOD AND BEER

Edelman's ability to successfully stage multinational P.R. campaigns wasn't limited just to emergencies. The agency stepped in to help several large companies as they fought to expand their business overseas.

During the reign of Mao Zedong, from 1949 to 1976, the government of China prohibited citizens from owning dogs as pets. Dogs were considered an indulgence and a threat to the country's food supply. But as China became more Westernized and affluent in the 1990s, the government eased its restrictions and dog ownership began to spread, especially among middle- and upper-class families.

Ocean. The temblor – the third strongest ever recorded – triggered a giant tsunami that killed more than a quarter of a million people in 14 Southeast Asian nations. It also instantly created more than 80,000 orphans. Edelman did pro bono work for Save the Children, an international relief organization that found itself overwhelmed with donations and offers of support.

Just a week after the tsunami, media had begun to question the activities of some NGOs involved in the relief effort, putting an immediate damper on donations. Save the Children wanted to avoid getting caught up in any such controversies and decided to tell the media and its donors in a compelling and transparent fashion what it was doing in the stricken areas.

To help them do so, Edelman donated more than $150,000 in services from its offices in Canada, Europe, Australia, the U.S., and Asia. The agency helped the charity produce print

Edelman client Mars Petcare – maker of such pet food brands as Royal Canin, Pedigree, and Whiskas – essentially created the Chinese pet care market, building a pet food factory in northern Beijing in 1995. To be successful, Mars knew it would need to educate Chinese officials and the public on the do's and don'ts of pet ownership – in a country where dogs are an occasional menu item.

Beginning in the mid-1990s, Edelman helped Mars stage a multifaceted P.R. campaign in Beijing and Shanghai. The effort included pet fairs on World Animal Day, where Chinese residents could see various dog breeds and query veterinarians. The agency also helped Mars pen an advice column that appeared regularly in hundreds of newspapers and worked with city governments to loosen local pet laws.

"The campaign was a foundational element to Mars operations in China, and it was a proven success," said Andrew Silver, who oversaw the Mars account as head of the Edelman Shanghai office. "Dog ownership has gone up every year since the beginning of the campaign, mirroring the rise of the Chinese middle class."

Other Edelman overseas campaigns involved alliances, including the 2004 merger of Belgium's Interbrew, the largest beer company in Europe, and Brazil's AmBev, the largest in South America. The beer companies joined to create InBev, the largest brewer in the world, with more than 200 brands (including such well-known names as Rolling Rock, Stella Artois, Skol, and Brahma), 70,000 employees, and operations in 35 countries.

David Brain first joined Edelman as head of the firm's operations in Europe, the Middle East, and Africa.

"They were facing a large internal communications challenge," said David Brain, who joined Edelman in 2003 as head of its European offices. "Interbrew and AmBev were two companies with distinct histories and distinct cultures and all their employees were wondering what was next."

After extensive research, Brain and Edelman helped launch InBev and its new, global culture, which they rolled out with the tagline "Your World's Premier Brewer." Key to the company's introduction was the involvement of employees, who appeared in internal company videos as well as external advertising.

GLOBAL TALENT SEARCH

Brain, a former journalist and P.R. executive at Weber Shandwick, joined Edelman after Richard reshuffled the European division in hopes of getting the offices to operate in a more coordinated fashion. "It was a bunch of offices that had never really worked together," said Brain. "They'd been losing money for three years.

"The first thing I did was to ask everyone in Europe to stop screwing up," he said with a laugh. "It was time to get back to basics. And that meant bringing in some new talent."

Brain strengthened the Edelman Europe offices with new hires and promotions, putting skilled managers in charge of key country operations, including Fiorella Passoni in Italy, Cornelia Kunze in Germany, and Annemieke Kievit in the Netherlands. Then Edelman made the biggest move in Europe in the company's history by purchasing Jackie Cooper Public Relations in London, Britain's leading consumer agency.

"Richard had tried to buy JCPR 10 years earlier," said Robert Phillips, JCPR cofounder. "I'll never forget the day he walked into the office back then. We were having a casting call for a client who sold brassieres and we had about 20 models walking around in their underwear."

Though Phillips and partner Jackie Cooper turned down Richard's offer in 1994, they called him a decade later to talk about joining forces. Brain led the negotiations for Edelman and the

JC Business

Jackie Cooper acquisition is good PR for Edelman

Joint campaign: Richard Edelman (centre) with Robert Phillips and Jackie Cooper from the newly acquired firm

Richard (center) with the cofounders of Jackie Cooper Public Relations, Robert Phillips (left) and Jackie Cooper.

two sides soon struck a deal. The acquisition of JCPR – with its 75 employees and clients such as Allied Domecq, Mary Kate & Ashley, and Wembley Stadium – greatly strengthened Edelman's position in the British P.R. market.

"ACT LIKE A REGION"

On the other side of the world, the Edelman operations were going through similar changes. Richard had tapped Alan VanderMolen – a former Burson-Marsteller executive who had competed against Edelman in Taiwan, Singapore, and Malaysia – to head the Asia Pacific offices. He inherited a market that had evolved significantly since

Dan had purchased Interasia in 1993. Especially in China.

"In the 1990s, P.R. firms placed Westerners in their Chinese offices, many of whom couldn't speak the language," said VanderMolen. "The firms needed to hire people who could speak the language, but the people studying Mandarin and Cantonese seemed to be more aligned with cultural studies and anthropology as opposed to business studies or journalism. So you ended up with great knowledge of basic cultural differences but not a tremendous amount of business depth."

As in Europe, while the Edelman offices in Asia experienced individual successes, they rarely acted in a coordinated manner. VanderMolen wanted to change that. "We had a simple, three-step plan when I went in: Think like a region, act like a region, lead the region," he said. Working from the Edelman Hong Kong office, VanderMolen convinced the leaders of the Asian offices to concentrate more on multinational business rather than accounts in their own countries. The strategy paid off, as the firm began to handle more Asia-wide P.R. campaigns for clients such as Microsoft, HP, and Starbucks, growing most quickly in work that involved digital communications.

Alan VanderMolen served for many years as head of the firm's operations in Asia Pacific.

TECHNOLOGY REDUX

If Edelman's first digital wave had begun with the work it did for Microsoft's Encarta on the Record and ended with the dot.com crash of 2001-2002, then the second wave began with the Pam Talbot-led campaign in support of Microsoft's Xbox video game console.

"We get to 2004 and we start to see some cool things bubble up," said Rick Murray, then head of the Edelman technology practice. "[Vermont] Governor Howard Dean starts raising large amounts of money for his campaign for president, five bucks at a time, over the Internet. Blogs explode in number and go from being geeky things to becoming common practices. MySpace is launched and people start to communicate in large numbers through social media.

"I came back from something called the Blog Business Summit in Seattle," continued Murray. "I was all fired up about the potential of blogging and social media. The classic response from 98 percent of the staff was: 'That's nice. You go do that.' But Richard and my boss, Nancy Ruscheinski, said, 'Let's go for it. What should we do?'"

With that, Edelman began to incorporate social media into a handful of its consumer campaigns with younger audiences, including efforts for Axe body spray and Microsoft's Xbox. Richard wanted to move more quickly and to more campaigns. "Richard told me, 'I want you to go out and reach P.R. bloggers in every market,'" Murray said. "I want you to go off and train our company. Talk to the clients. Get people believing. Evangelize!'"

Richard joined the believers in September 2004 when he did something no other CEO of a large public relations firm had ever attempted. He started his own blog, calling it 6 A.M.

"Why 6 A.M.?" Richard wrote in his first post. "Because I wake up early and hope to get you some useful insights as you come in to work. Just a few rules for me. Don't expect any shortened phrases like GTG or 4U. I will tell you as much as I can about specific issues but sometimes I will not be able to tell you everything. And I want feedback, blunt and quick."

In Richard's first posts he talked about his business meetings, foreign travels, and items from the day's news that he wanted to share. He opined on ethics in P.R. and mourned a friend who had committed suicide. The format seemed to turn Richard into a modern-day version of his

Richard has been a prodigious blogger since September 2004, sharing opinions and experiences from his professional life as well as his personal one.

correspondence-happy father, penning notes that blended business tips and personal stories. It was Dan Edelman 2.0.

In one post, Richard called the increasing demand for interactive communications the "me-too revolution." The phrase became the name for the Edelman digital practice headed by Murray. "Some people thought the name was silly, but I didn't care," said Murray. "We accomplished exactly what we wanted to do, and that was not only to build a successful digital practice but to actually digitize the firm."

Murray's growing team began to influence all Edelman practices and offices. Edelman became the first large P.R. firm to build client presences on MySpace. The digital division developed social media press releases, which contained text, videos, images, and links, all search engine-optimized. Phil Gomes, a blogger from San Francisco and Murray's first hire, created a social media "belt" hierarchy similar to that found in the martial arts. Employees who mastered more complex social media techniques were awarded higher-level belts.

MAJOR DIVIDENDS

Richard's flurry of moves during 2002-2005 were a huge gamble for Edelman, both internally and with clients. Historically, corporations had resisted P.R. activities that required them to reveal what was considered to be proprietary information. Now, here was a man telling them they needed to open up, be transparent; to admit mistakes when they were wrong, and behave more like friendly neighbors than business operations with an eye only on the bottom line. Misgivings aside, the vast majority of Edelman's clients began to embrace the new approach.

Likewise, Richard's human resources initiatives and operational overhauls could have been rejected by staff members. In fact, some employees did bristle after being told they were going to be rated by clients on their work or forced to act less like a member of an office and more as a member of a region. But most staffers, seeing that the new initiatives were beginning to pay off in client satisfaction and increasing revenues, applauded the changes.

Perhaps the biggest move Richard made during this period was his decision – like that of his father – to reject purchase offers and keep Edelman independent and privately owned.

Independence. A more coordinated, global and regional approach. An emphasis on quality. The growth of Edelman's digital operation. And the firm's emergence as provider of intellectual property with its Trust Barometer. Richard's initiatives, though chancy when first unveiled, now began to pay off in a big way.

"When we started to get clients like GE and Walmart, that's when we knew the worm had turned," said Richard, who credits Leslie Dach for the new business.

A WORLD OF ECOMAGINATION

Edelman had conducted hundreds of major launches in its 50-plus year history, but none had as high stakes as the work the agency did to support GE's unveiling of ecomagination, the manufacturer's new initiative that promoted clean technologies, including hybrid railroad locomotives and fuel efficient airplane engines. The announcement marked a major policy and positioning change for GE, and the company knew it would be greeted with skepticism from some activists who pointed to the company's record on the environment (in particular, its role in polluting the Hudson River with PCBs) and shareholders who questioned if the company's trying to look ecologically responsible made good business sense.

ecomagination℠

On May 9, 2005, General Electric unveiled ecomagination, an initiative to bring to market new technologies that will help customers meet pressing environmental challenges. Jeffrey Immelt, GE chairman and CEO, spoke at a news conference; Jonathan Lash, president of the World Resources Institute, joined him on stage.

magazine cover story headline. *U.S. News and World Report* credited GE for being able to "shift the political landscape in favor of action on climate change."

SAVE MONEY. LIVE BETTER.

When Walmart hired Edelman in 2005, the retailing giant was in the middle of fending off a well-organized anti-Walmart campaign financed largely by labor unions. Activists across the country had been taking swipes at the company, whose associates (employees) were non-unionized. They were organizing boycotts, staging protest events,

Working with GE for more than a year researching opinions, refining messages, and building coalitions, Edelman helped the company position ecomagination as an effort that was good for both the environment and the company's bottom line.

For the ecomagination launch event, Edelman chose an auditorium at the George Washington University School of Business in the nation's capital to support the idea that the initiative was serious policy. The agency helped arrange for a bevy of scholars, environmentalists, government officials, and business leaders to be on hand, including Jonathan Lash, CEO of the World Resources Institute, who shared the stage with Immelt and gave an honest assessment of ecomagination and its value to the planet.

GE received near universal acclaim for ecomagination, including coverage in most leading business media outlets. "GE Goes Green," said a *Forbes*

and generally behaving as if they were in the middle of a heated political campaign.

In response, Edelman and Walmart adopted a campaign-style approach as well. They set up a rapid response unit of staffers at Walmart headquarters in Bentonville, Arkansas, in a room they called Action Alley. The team began to answer charges with fact sheets, statements, and interviews that helped to set the record straight. When opponents released a critical movie, the team countered with its own film that pointed out the factual errors and distortions in the "documentary."

In future years, the Edelman work with Walmart evolved from critical response to proactive outreach. Edelman assisted the retailer in efforts to communicate with media and consumers interested in its efforts on such issues as health care and the environment. The agency

START YOUR OWN HEDGE FUND · THE FUTURE OF COMPUTING

FORTUNE

WAL-MART SAVES THE PLANET

Well, not quite. But CEO LEE SCOTT's green campaign, which started as PR, is becoming a force of nature.

"What I thought was going to be a defensive strategy is turning out to be precisely the opposite."

DISPLAY UNTIL AUGUST 14, 2006

Since 2005, Edelman has helped Walmart communicate a number of significant programs, including its $4 prescription drug program and its efforts to make healthful food more affordable and accessible.

helped Walmart roll out its $4 prescription drug program as well as initiatives that support sustainability. Edelman also played a major role helping Walmart expand its web and social media presence, providing consumers with more opportunities to share their opinions.

Edelman also provides P.R. support for Walmart's efforts to make healthful foods more afford-able and more accessible, by helping build and drive engagement with key influencers, food and nutrition experts, and ultimately its cus-tomers through such groups as Partnership for a Healthier America, a nonprofit organization fighting child obesity that is chaired by first lady Michelle Obama.

6 A.M.

Since 2004, Richard has shared his opinions and experiences in his weekly blog, called 6 A.M. Here are some brief samples of his musings.

We should not take on any client in the way that a lawyer can claim that every client deserves representation. . . . We need to be utterly trans-parent in our work methods. . . . We should demand a seat at the decision-making table and not simply accept the role of mouthpiece for legal counsel.
November 29, 2004 – On the role of P.R.

There is new technology that can help men make better decisions about treatment. It is important for men to realize that the treatment options will not affect their quality of life in the long run.
March 31, 2009 – Among the many reasons Richard gave for going public with the news of his prostate cancer.

I am ultimately going to turn the reins at Edel-man over to my three daughters, whether as owners or managers. They will have to make their own decisions about work/life balance, about the right life partners and about where to live. What I want for them and for all of the women at Edelman is that they make the call about how far and how fast they want to rise in the organization and that they have the op-portunity to thrive without having to choose between Edelman and life outside of work.
September 1, 2011 – Introducing Global Women Executive Network [GWEN], an internal task force to address the challenges women face in the workplace.

Empathy and humanity are what people remember, not the numbers.
October 7, 2011 – Richard reflecting on his tenure as CEO.

CHAPTER 13

PUBLIC ENGAGEMENT

Richard's series of high-stakes maneuvers after 9/11 – his emphasis on a global approach and quality service, his investment in technology and social media, his decision to keep the firm independent, his moves to develop intellectual property, and his advocacy for corporations to engage in two-way, transparent communication – paid off with larger clients and greater revenues.

The Holmes Report, which, like the Harris/Impulse Survey, had criticized Edelman for its hit-and-miss work just a few years earlier, now presented Edelman with its 2005 International Agency of the Year award, citing, among other things, the growth in Europe and Asia under David Brain and Alan VanderMolen, respectively.

But a more interesting transformation was also taking place. Edelman campaigns were changing in tone and scope, tackling issues society often ignored and expanding the boundaries of traditional public relations. When Edelman unveiled a thought-provoking campaign on behalf of a brand known best for its soap, the rest of the world could see the evolution as well.

THE VOICE OF MEDIA   VOL. LIII   NO. 3   REPRINTED FROM JANUARY 23-29, 2012

ADWEEK

PR Agency

AGENCY OF THE YEAR

President and CEO **Richard Edelman** and U.S. president and CEO **Matthew Harrington.**

Photo: Ben Shaul

Richard's high stakes gambles paid off in numerous honors, including Agency of the Year from *AdWeek*.

GETTING REAL

For generations, personal-care and beauty supply companies used young and slender, Hollywood-style models in their advertising and marketing campaigns. But when Dove (Unilever) was ready to launch a new line of products called Dove Firming, it wanted to take a different approach; one that expanded that limited definition of beauty. It hired Edelman to lead the public relations component for a global advertising, P.R., and marketing campaign that was to be called the Dove Campaign for Real Beauty.

To begin the effort, Dove and Edelman's StrategyOne research arm conducted a 10-country survey that uncovered some alarming results. Only 2 percent of the respondents described themselves as "beautiful," while only 13 percent were satisfied with their weight and shape. The respondents felt the mass media set unrealistic standards of beauty that few women could ever achieve.

Armed with the results, Edelman organized a series of a series of product events in Europe using a group of amateur models of all shapes and sizes. Often they were clad in nothing but their underwear in an effort to get people talking about and debating society's beauty standards. The events struck a chord with women and earned an unprecedented amount of media coverage for a product launch.

Expanding the Campaign for Real Beauty to the U.S., Edelman coordinated a multi-month-long media tour that landed Real Beauty campaign models on such national television shows as *Oprah*, *Ellen*, *Dr. Phil*, and *The Today Show*, as well as on the cover of *People* magazine, among thousands of media placements. Similar efforts took place around the world.

In future years the Dove Campaign for Real Beauty evolved to feature women over the age of 50 and promote self-esteem among girls around the world through conferences, social media programs, and support of such organizations as the Girl Scouts and Boys and Girls Clubs. The campaign, which is still going strong, has helped millions of people realize that the real definition of beauty comes from within.

HEART TO HEART

There was also another organization that wanted to change public perceptions – the American Heart Association. Heart disease is the No. 1 killer of women in America, claiming one in three lives. Yet, according to AHA polling, most women believed that heart disease was something that happened to somebody else.

Edelman helped personalize that risk when it joined with the AHA to conduct a campaign about the dangers of heart disease not through the use of statistics but through telling real-life stories of everyday women who survived heart attacks and other heart ailments. Edelman

The Dove Campaign for Real Beauty began with an international survey conducted by StrategyOne, Edelman's research arm, and featured "real women" in its advertising and P.R. activities.

also created an online tool it called the Go Red Heart CheckUp, which allowed women to gauge their risk of heart attack, as well as an online forum that encouraged women to share their stories.

The agency partnered with NBC to produce a nationally syndicated documentary that followed the lives of women recovering from heart disease and signed up Marie Osmond, whose mother and grandmother had died of heart disease, as the national campaign spokesperson. More than one million women took the Go Read Heart CheckUp online and more than 220,000 registered with the American Heart Association for additional information about heart disease.

COMMUNITY ACTION

While campaigns like the ones for Dove and the AHA helped build and empower communities of people, other Edelman efforts shaped communities of place. For instance, in 2005 the Edelman Travel and Hospitality group helped turn Springfield, Illinois, into a must-visit destination with a P.R. campaign that supported the opening of the new Abraham Lincoln Presidential Library and Museum. Several years later, it did the same for the Gettysburg National Battlefield and its new on-site museum. Richard, a Civil War buff since the age of six, helped raise awareness for the historic Pennsylvania site as a member of the Gettysburg Foundation.

Another community building effort focused on the environment. Masdar, a 2.25-square-mile planned development in the United Arab Emirates' capital, Abu Dhabi, is described as the world's first zero-carbon city. The future home to 45,000 residents and 1,500 clean-tech companies,

Masdar – *masdar* means "the source" in Arabic – relies on renewable energy for power and transports residents in driverless electric vehicles that buzz through underground tunnels.

Edelman helped introduce Masdar to the world in 2006, while at the same time positioning Abu Dhabi – indeed the entire UAE – as a hub for clean energy innovation as well as investment. In addition to a series of launch events and global media efforts, Edelman organized the first-ever World Future Energy Summit, an event that attracted 11,000 participants and 85 speakers, one of whom was Britain's Prince Charles. Agency efforts landed Masdar on CNN, BBC, and Al Jazeera, as well as in *The New York Times*, *Time* magazine, the *Financial Times*, and many other publications.

Back in the Western Hemisphere, Edelman helped the Panama Canal Authority address lingering global skepticism over the U.S. handover

Masdar, in Abu Dhabi, is described as the world's first zero-carbon city. Edelman helped bring it to the world's attention through media efforts, launch events, and the first-ever World Future Energy Summit.

of the canal to Panama in advance of a hoped-for multibillion-dollar expansion.

The canal sought to add a third lane and expand the locks to allow the passage of bigger ships, a much-needed enhancement that would require billions of dollars, significant education of the global trade and shipping community, and the approval of a majority of the citizens of Panama. Some doubted Panama's ability to run the canal and felt it might squander resources for short-term gain. (In reality, the Panamanians run the canal better than the United States ever did.)

Deaver's strategic counsel was essential to Edelman's campaign to position and promote the canal and the expansion. The project needed the unofficial imprimatur of the shipping community and approval in a popular referendum. Edelman wanted to come up with a tagline that would help put things the best possible light.

After extensive research and brainstorming, Edelman staffers sat down to try to come up with a tagline. "Mike Deaver sat at the table and listened intently for about an hour," said Richard. "Then he leaned forward and said calmly, 'Let's try to simplify things and just say – The New Panama Canal: A Better Way to Go.'"

Deaver's suggestion would become Edelman's campaign slogan. It crisply summarized Panama's successful stewardship of the waterway and the many benefits of expansion, including increased jobs and commerce. In October 2006, 76 percent of Panamanians voted to approve the expansion of the canal.

BLUE RIBBON ADVICE

Before Mike Deaver joined Edelman in 1992, many people in Washington, D.C., had dismissed him due to his legal troubles since leaving the White House. But Deaver proved his

Mike Deaver, who had served in President Reagan's White House, joined Edelman in 1992 and brought wisdom and gravitas to the firm. He counseled clients and mentored staffers, always allowing others to enjoy the spotlight.

naysayers wrong. He was seen increasingly as one of the most talented and successful professionals to ever work in the field of agency public relations.

In the aftermath of 9/11, President George W. Bush called for a commission of senior statesmen to examine the "circumstances surrounding the September 11 attacks." Chaired by former New Jersey Governor Thomas Kean, a Republican, and vice-chaired by former Congressman Lee Hamilton, a Democrat, the 10-member commission spent 19 months interviewing witnesses and rooting out failures in the nation's preparedness. It also came up with a bipartisan plan to attempt to thwart similar attacks in the future. But without an aggressive P.R. push, commission members worried that their findings and recommendations would fall on deaf ears. They wanted to pressure Congress and the Bush administration to enact their proposals. They called Mike Deaver and Edelman.

When the 9/11 Commission was ready to release its report, Edelman organized a media push that began with a press conference, then moved on to three days of media interviews with commissioners in the Edelman offices, and continued with a 10-city national media tour.

Deaver later convinced the commission to turn itself into a nonprofit organization so that it could raise money and continue to advocate on behalf of its recommendations. The commission took his advice, and Edelman helped the group stage media events to report on the progress of the 9/11 proposals. In the end, the 9/11 Commission report became one of the year's best-selling publications.

Deaver, colleague Rob Rehg, and Edelman D.C. performed a similar task for the Iraq Study Group, a 10-person bipartisan panel appointed by Congress in 2006 to examine America's military engagement in Iraq. An Edelman media blitz helped convince journalists and the public that the group's report was a thoughtful and non-political blueprint for improving the situation in Iraq. Chairman James Baker, the former secretary of state who had served with Deaver in the Reagan administration, said that Deaver's leadership gave both Democrats and Republicans on the task force confidence that its findings would receive a full and fair hearing.

TECH RAMP-UP

The firm's growing strength in technology was key to the success of many of its efforts. A couple of high-visibility campaigns in the mid-2000s distinguished Edelman as a leader in the tech P.R. field: the launch of the hit video game Halo-2 and the unveiling of Microsoft's Xbox 360, the successor to the first Xbox game console.

In both efforts, Edelman connected with millions of video gamers around the world through creative Internet activities and local events and promotions staged by offices in Asia, Europe, and North America. The firm was carving out a new model, one that blended traditional P.R. techniques with emerging technologies.

Edelman Germany came up with a creative idea based on new Internet applications when it was handed the assignment of promoting a dental care product for dogs called Pedigree DentaStix. Instead of focusing exclusively on the product, Edelman launched a dating website . . . for dogs. "Social media in Germany was in its infant shoes, and this was a first-of-its-kind campaign – certainly for dogs," said then Edelman Germany chief Cornelia Kunze. "The media jumped all over it. They were reporting the story for more than a year after the campaign was over."

Edelman had been on a digital media worker hiring spree since the economy had begun to recover in 2004, though its new employees tended to be bloggers and technology P.R. specialists rather than computer programmers or digital artists. Those hirings were to pay off in a big way with the burgeoning of social media.

"MySpace, Facebook, and Twitter made Edelman the perfect digital firm, because companies no longer needed people to create programs, they needed content providers," said Richard. "We were there. Ahead of all the other P.R. firms."

Richard and Pam Talbot joined the senior team of A&R shortly after Edelman acquired the Silicon Valley-based tech firm. From left, John Derryberry, Richard, Talbot, Maria Amundson, Lisa Auslen, Zelda Rudin, Bob Angus, and Todd Irwin.

With the firm's digital workload beginning to skyrocket, Edelman beefed up its technology practice even further, hiring dozens of social media experts, including Steve Rubel, the nation's premier advertising blogger. The digital practice went to work crafting word-of-mouth and social media campaigns for Edelman's biggest clients.

Then Edelman made an even bolder technology move. It purchased Silicon Valley-based A&R Partners, a technology P.R. firm with 115 employees and an all-star client list that included Adobe, Mozilla, and Palm. Overnight the merged firm, now called A&R Edelman, became a top P.R. firm in Silicon Valley and other tech centers across the country. The acquisition helped boost Edelman revenues to more than $300 million annually and made technology the third-largest practice at the firm, behind only the health care and consumer practices. It also enabled Edelman to win HP's global PC business the following year.

Two years later, Edelman, in an effort led by UK head Robert Phillips, purchased London-based Spook Media, a digital P.R. firm. The move jumpstarted Edelman's digital business in the UK, adding 15 digital specialists to the London office along with clients like Seiko, the Excel Exhibition Centre, and the Fashion Targets Breast Cancer organization. Phillips positioned the Spook unit in the front of the redesigned Edelman London office, a signal to staff and clients that digital was at the heart of most Edelman campaigns.

CHANGING OF THE GUARD

As the company was expanding its digital practice the firm itself underwent some significant changes in leadership. In 2006, Michael Morley, who in 1967 had opened Edelman's

first office abroad and then gone on to help turn the firm into a global P.R. powerhouse, retired as deputy chairman.

Shortly thereafter, Leslie Dach departed to take a job as executive vice president, corporate affairs for Walmart. Dach had been responsible for building the agency's highly regarded global public affairs practice and shaping the Edelman Washington, D.C., office into the top agency in town.

Dan turned 86 on July 3, 2006. His body, still sinewy and trim thanks to a lifetime of healthful eating and lots of exercise, began to slow down. But he talked with Richard by phone every day to catch up on the latest company news and he still went to the office regularly, giving advice when he thought it would be helpful.

Dan and Ruth spent more time together. In a video interview, he reflected on their 50-plus year partnership and what she meant to the firm. "Ruth has absolutely been a model of what is needed by somebody who was trying to build a business as I was," he said. "She's just been a great person in terms of relationships with

Ruth and Dan, circa 1992.

people. I wouldn't have any friends. Literally. She's very outgoing and sociable. She likes people; and she does things for people. People go to her when they're getting a divorce, or when they have a death in the family.

"And Ruth has always had great ideas about business. She majored in economics at the University of Wisconsin. She's very smart. When she comes up with something that's a good idea, she'll tell me or Richard. She does that all the time. So if we've [Edelman] been successful she deserves a great amount of credit for what we've been able to accomplish."

Together, Dan and Ruth attended as many Edelman gatherings as possible. They traveled to Washington, D.C., in June 2007 so that Dan could address company executives at an Edelman Global Leadership meeting. In the hotel room the afternoon before the meeting, Dan fell ill and was not going to be able to attend the event. He asked Michael Deaver to step in to take his place.

"As I began to think about the task and what to say," said Deaver to Edelman's senior management. "I began to realize that I have spent my entire professional life working for two men . . . Ronald Reagan for 20 years and Dan Edelman for 16 years . . . and in so many ways, they were the same.

"They both were great communicators. Both understood the importance of having good and talented people around them. Both were 'Davids' for much of their careers and were underestimated, but both were driven to succeed and did so beyond their expectations. Both knew who they were and were comfortable in their own skin. And finally both had a code of ethics and values that were and are unshakable.

"Know who you are. Be open and transparent. Be ready for change. These three values easily

describe Edelman today. We are on the verge of something great. Let's not forget the values that got us here today."

What Michael Deaver didn't mention that evening was the fact he was losing his battle with pancreatic cancer. Less than two months later, he died at his home in Bethesda, Maryland.

Dan, Richard, and the rest of the company took Michael Deaver's death hard. The man had become the soul of Edelman, a wise professional to clients and a mentor to many young staffers. He gave the firm gravitas and guidance. Now he was gone.

"Mike Deaver was, at his core, a decent, hardworking American, a family man whose reality of goodness and integrity in the end is much more important than his legendary mastery of the photo opportunity," said Richard at Deaver's memorial service.

Only one person left at Edelman matched Deaver for his impact and importance – U.S. CEO Pam Talbot. In nearly four decades of service at the firm, Talbot had crafted many of Edelman's most iconic campaigns, while also serving as mentor and inspiration to generations of Edelman employees. Whenever Edelman faced a major challenge it turned to Pam Talbot. She led the company's efforts to improve its work quality and global client management. At her urging, more and more Edelman campaigns addressed greater societal goods.

While her last name wasn't Edelman, Pam Talbot was considered family. So when she told Richard she planned to retire in 2008, it felt to him as if he was losing a sister at work.

"I look at this company today and literally feel . . . out of breath," wrote Pam in her farewell memo to the staff. "Together we've come so far, so fast. Yes, with confusion and missteps. And certainly with miles to go. But there's no question we've run faster and smarter than our peer set." (See sidebar "Farewell Advice from a Master," page 163.)

Fueled by digital media and business abroad, Edelman was in the middle of a period of exponential growth. By the end of 2008, Edelman employed 3,400 people in 54 offices, including new offices in Orlando, Berlin, Abu Dhabi, and Warsaw. The firm had finally opened a profitable office in Tokyo, erasing the memory of several failed attempts in previous years in that city. Edelman seemed to be making all the right moves and reported revenues of nearly $450 million.

While there was plenty of good news to share, Richard suddenly felt alone. Gone were the titans of the firm, his idols, the people who had built Edelman from a small, Chicago-based consumer agency into a major international P.R. player with multiple specialties and a full head of steam.

A NEW GENERATION CARRIES ON

But there was no turning back. At the end of the decade, Richard looked to a new generation of executives to carry on the Edelman tradition –

To celebrate the launch of Pike Place Roast, Edelman created – in New York City's Bryant Park – a replica of the original Starbucks store in Seattle's Pike Place Market.

people like Matt Harrington, president of the New York office; and Victor Malanga, chief financial officer; David Brain, president of the European region and Alan VanderMolen, Brain's counterpart in Asia; Julianna Richter, president of global client relationship management; and Gail Becker, president of the western U.S. region.

And carry it on they did. Led by a new breed of executives, the company continued to implement innovative campaigns that incorporated Edelman's classic attributes and new strengths of technology, global reach, and public engagement. Increasingly, Edelman became the go-to firm for multinational companies or organizations with large P.R. needs.

After years of record growth, Starbucks faced a series of challenges in early 2008, including increasing competition and falling stock prices. Starbucks chairman, Howard Schultz, returned as CEO and decided that the company needed to go back to its roots with a renewed focus on its premium coffee and the communities in which it operated. Starbucks called on Edelman to help promote the new approach.

The Starbucks transformation began with the introduction of Pike Place Roast, named after the company's original store in Seattle's Pike Place Market and created based on characteristics customers said were most important to them: taste, freshness, and quality. Edelman, led by Amy Kavanaugh, coordinated simultaneous launch events in New York – where it constructed a replica of the original Pike Place Market store – and Seattle, generating significant media coverage and a positive online buzz, making Pike Place Roast the No. 1 Google search term on the day of the events.

Shortly thereafter, Starbucks closed all company-operated stores in the U.S. to conduct a three-and-a-half-hour in-store event they called "Espresso Excellence Training" for more than 135,000 baristas, which Starbucks calls partners.

Edelman offices across the country handled media relations for the unprecedented event, setting up a hotline to field more than 300 media requests and placing the story in hundreds of media outlets, including *The New York Times*, *The Wall Street Journal*, NPR, nightly network newscasts, and even humorous segments on Comedy Central's *The Daily Show* and *The Colbert Report*. "If getting the message across to tens of millions counts for anything, Starbucks, long a believer in P.R. rather than advertising, hit this one out of the park," said *Advertising Age* of the event.

In an effort to reduce the use of disposable water containers, the Brita FilterForGood campaign offers free filtered water at concerts and other events.

Three years later, more than 20 Edelman offices worldwide helped Starbucks celebrate its 40th anniversary with the unveiling of its new brand featuring the iconic Starbucks Siren, multiple product launches, and support for more than 2,000 community service projects around the world for a "Global Month of Service." The anniversary was the largest and most far-reaching P.R. campaign ever staged by Starbucks and Edelman. Following the celebration, Starbucks saw record third quarter results as well as media coverage that reached more than 2.7 billion people in 24 countries.

"ME" TO "WE"

Around the world, more large companies were adopting the strategy Richard had outlined years earlier in his paper "The Relationship Imperative." They were moving away from top-down communications to a more cooperative approach that the firm referred to as "public engagement." They listened to customers who wanted to support products that contributed to a greater societal good. At Edelman, through digital or live activities and events, clients were helped to make the transition from "me" to "we," finding areas of mutual interest where companies could help address community needs while also enhancing their bottom lines.

In one such instance, the Brita water filter maker, with Edelman's help and counsel, launched an effort called FilterForGood. Among other things, this initiative offered free filtered water at concerts and other large gatherings; this not only showed off the product but also decreased the use of throw-away plastic bottles. Charmin set up free toilets in various New York City locations to point out the chronic lack of such public facilities in the city. In Chicago, Stove Top Stuffing sponsored an effort to provide winter heat to bus shelters. Edelman offices provided P.R. support for all of these initiatives.

The public engagement approach expanded to other parts of the Edelman network. On behalf of Unilever's Dirt is Good campaign, an effort to promote outdoor play for children, Edelman London/Jackie Cooper P.R. has produced a series of short films that demonstrate fun new activities that also educate kids about subjects like conservation and recycling. The films have been shown throughout Western Europe, South America, and Vietnam, the latter of which has added recess to school curriculums as a result of the Dirt is Good campaign.

While most Edelman campaigns took months of planning and research, sometimes they struck without warning.

On June 1, 2009, Edelman Brazil president Ronald Mincheff received a phone call at 5:30 in the morning from a distraught client at Air France. One of the airline's planes, en route from Rio de Janeiro to Paris, had crashed into the Atlantic during the night, killing all 228 people on board. Sobbing, she asked for help from Edelman to answer the hundreds of media inquiries that were flooding in.

Mincheff immediately dispatched teams to the Rio airport, to the Air France office in São Paolo, and to a hotel in Rio where a bereavement center for families of the victims was being set up. The Edelman teams helped Air France officials brief media on the latest developments.

A month after the crash, Mincheff and the Edelman offices in São Paolo and Rio de Janeiro hosted a gathering to unveil a memorial statue to honor the 228 passengers and crew members lost on the flight.

"The event was the first moment when the extended families were brought together to have their loved ones remembered and honored," said Mincheff. "It was an emotional event that helped the healing process while marking that catastrophic, lonely moment that transpired in the dark of night and in the middle of the ocean."

AND THEN ONE DAY IT HAPPENED

After 58 years in operation, Edelman was red hot.

Its work included everything from putting a human face on Big Oil for the American Petroleum Institute to helping Trojan brand condoms become a leading authority on sexual health. For eBay, Edelman set up a temporary store in midtown Manhattan during the Christmas holiday season and, in a separate event, rolled out a promotion with a theme based on the classic television game show *Let's Make a Deal* to let the world know that eBay was a shop-ping destination for new items, not just for collectibles and people's cast-offs.

Edelman's digital business continued to soar. When Wonderbra introduced a lingerie line designed by burlesque performer Dita Von Teese, the P.R. campaign didn't rely on press releases or launch events; instead it featured online photos and a short video of Von Teese in the sexy lingerie. The video went viral and the Von Teese line sold out within two weeks.

And then one day it happened.

In early 2011, Edelman became the largest public relations firm in the world. According to *PR Week* and *Advertising Age*, the firm, nearly six decades old, with revenues topping a half-billion dollars, had moved past Weber Shandwick, Fleishman-Hillard, and Burson-Marsteller to assume the P.R. world's top position.

"Independence won," declared Jack O'Dwyer, publisher of "Jack O'Dwyer's Newsletter," a P.R. industry report. "Edelman was the only big firm that stayed true to the craft and didn't sell out."

Dan's dream, hatched in a small Chicago office in 1952 with a staff of three, nurtured by a roster of talented practitioners, and carried to fruition by the hard work and key decisions of his older son, had come true.

In typical Edelman style, there was little fanfare. Richard said he is sure he talked to Dan about the news, but neither man remembers the conversation. If anything, both Edelmans rejected the crown.

Dan used the opportunity to reiterate one of his well-known sayings: "It's great to be the biggest P.R. firm, but I always want to be the best."

Richard acknowledged the victory, then reset the race. "Edelman's DNA is entrepreneurial, aggressive, feisty, and ambitious," he wrote in his blog. "How could I square this circle [of becoming No. 1], I wondered, and recognize the achievement but maintain the underdog mentality."

The solution to that conundrum hit him during a visit he made to the American Museum of Natural History in New York. During the visit a friend pointed out the Morganucodon, or Morgie, a shrewlike creature that evolved from reptiles during the Late Triassic period, about 205 million years ago. The Morganucodon survived the extinction event that wiped out the dinosaurs and became the earliest common ancestor to all future mammals, including humans. Yes, thought Richard. Edelman was like the Morgie.

Not long after this epiphany, Richard shared the analogy with senior staff members at an Edelman meeting in London. "We were written off a decade ago because we decided to remain independent, bucking the trend of holding company ownership," he said. "Then we went against trend again to compete aggressively in the digital business. We are operating in a moment similar to the time when the great meteorite hit the earth, setting off a huge extinction of the creatures that had been dominant up to that point. And now, the little Morgie has grown up into the leader of the P.R. business."

The crowd erupted with laughter, then nodded in agreement. They knew that while the firm had reached a milestone as the world's top P.R. agency, the big competition in future years would come from different quarters, including advertising companies, digital agencies, and consulting firms. To thrive, they would need to adapt. They were all going to have to be Morgies from now on.

FAREWELL ADVICE FROM A MASTER

When she retired from Edelman in 2008, U.S. CEO Pam Talbot shared 10 hard-won lessons with her colleagues.

Work from the horizon in. Have an expansive view of where you want your career to go, all the way to the horizon. And know that there are many ways to get there.

Tilt toward "yes." Always lean forward – that's where the possibilities are.

Have a sense of humor. When you see the humor in things, you're more likely to see the solution.

Channel Shakespeare. Look to your supporters to turn your ideas into reality; to your doubters to make you smarter and more thoughtful; and to your enemies to make you tougher.

Know your weaknesses, but play to your strengths. Recognize what you do better than anyone else around you – and surround yourself with people who can shore up what you don't do as well.

Winning takes forever; losing takes a moment. Every client needs to be won and re-won every week.

See windows, not walls. Our job has always been to connect our clients to the bigger world.

Play to please yourself. Respect how other people see you and rate your performance, but be your own fiercest critic and greatest fan.

Have the humility to recognize you might not always have the right answer, the wisdom to engage lots of brains, and the courage to express a point of view no matter whom you're talking to.

Oddly, business is about love. You can't lead without loving the people you're leading and loving the work you do.

EPILOGUE

On a misty autumn morning in 2012, students at the Columbia Journalism School idled between classes on an outdoor plaza near a café in the newly constructed student center. They read *The New York Times*, sipped coffee, and talked about a world of big stories waiting to be told.

Their gathering spot is a place of ideas and dreams, a respite from classroom rigors. It is named for an alumnus and benefactor who, through a combination of journalism training and a passion for business, created the largest and most successful public relations firm in the world. It is the Daniel J. Edelman Plaza.

In recognition of a lifetime of professional achievement and civic involvement, the Columbia Journalism School presented Dan with its first-ever Dean's Medal for Public Service. "There could be no better initial recipient than Daniel Edelman, who is both a world leader in his field and an outstandingly generous and public-spirited man," said dean Nicholas Lemann in announcing the award.

It seems most fitting for Dan to support a practice that he's admired since boyhood. "I still quietly edit *The New York Times, USA Today,* and the *Chicago Tribune* and rewrite the headlines in my head. I have this journalism thing in my blood," he said. "But public relations has been very rewarding. I feel good about having played an important role in the development of what is in fact still a new field."

The 21st century has brought many honors for Dan Edelman. In September 2007, Richard spoke about his father at the unveiling of a plaque in Dan's honor at the Aon Center in Chicago.

Dan shakes hands with Nicholas Lemann, dean of the Graduate School of Journalism at Columbia University, after being awarded the Dean's Medal for Public Service.

KEYS TO SUCCESS

On October 1, 2012, the agency that Dan founded turned 60. Richard traveled to the Edelman Chicago office for an anniversary lunch and a teleconference with staff around the world. Dan, hospitalized with a variety of ailments, was unable to attend. "My father developed a set of operating principles for the firm," Richard said. "Hire the best talent, and retain them by giving them the chance to be entrepreneurial. Invest in proprietary intellectual capital . . . and give clients access to it. Expand in new markets by reinvesting all of your earnings each year. Never take on debt. Remain independent and family-owned, so that you serve no one's interests but those of your clients. And for 60 years, these principles have not changed."

Most of the people working at Edelman today have never had the opportunity of meeting Dan in person. Instead they know him through the ethos of the organization. They see Dan's personality each time they come up with a creative idea that wows a client and each time they work late to prepare for a big event. They know him by the ethical standards he set for the office and the field of public relations.

"Today, with 65 offices, 4,500 employees, and $637 million in revenue, we are the world's largest P.R. firm thanks to Dan's foundational values," said Richard.

Edelman now has a more extensive worldwide network than any other firm in the field. Between 2010 and 2012, Edelman opened offices in Calgary, Dubai, Moscow, and five new branches in India – Ahmedabad, Chennai, Hyderabad, Kolkata, and Pune. It acquired Vollmer P.R., the largest independent firm in Houston; AVC Communications in Ho Chi Minh City, Vietnam; Zurich-based K Comms; and Significa, the leading brand marketing firm in Brazil.

Edelman's independent and debt-free status has allowed it to move quickly to acquire firms and open offices. After David Brain, then head of Edelman operations in Europe, the Middle East, and Africa, on a 2008 visit to Abu Dhabi received assurances for significant new business in that city, he called Richard from a taxi. "I told him we had some great opportunities and that I needed $300,000 to open an office. There was a brief pause, then he said, 'Do it.' We were up and running in no

Victor Malanga, Edelman's chief financial officer.

In 2012, Richard Edelman appointed Matthew Harrington Global Chief Operating Officer. Harrington first joined Edelman in 1984.

time, and it's been one of our most successful new offices."

In 2012, Richard strengthened his leadership team by naming Matthew Harrington to the position of chief operating officer, the firm's second in command. Meanwhile, Alan Vander-Molen was promoted to vice chairman of the Daniel J. Edelman family of companies (which now also includes the sports and marketing firm Matter) and CEO of the firm's global practices. David Brain shifted from overseeing European operations to president and CEO of Edelman Asia Pacific. They were joined on the Edelman Executive Committee by Victor Malanga, chief financial officer; Gail Becker, chair of Edelman Canada and Latin America; Mark Hass, president and CEO of Edelman U.S.; Robert Phillips, president and CEO of Edelman Europe; and Julianna Richter, president of global client relationship management.

John Edelman is spearheading an effort to support Edelman's corporate citizenship. In September 2012, his team launched a microsite called FY'12 Citizenship Report: It's Who We Are to illustrate the firm's efforts to engage with its communities, support organizations through volunteerism, and limit its carbon footprint and greenhouse gas emissions.

"Edelman employees have been involved with community organizations and causes since the day my father founded the firm," said John. "Now, in this era of public engagement, Edelman is intent on doing even more in the communities it serves."

Edelman has always believed that its employees are, by far, the agency's top resource. And just as computer companies invest in technology and pharmaceutical companies spend significant amounts on research and development, Edelman invests in its people.

As managing director of Global Engagement and Corporate Responsibility, John Edelman is leading the firm's sustainability and community outreach efforts.

GLOBAL GOOD

The rapid growth that Edelman has seen around the world has required the firm to take steps to establish a common corporate culture and ensure that all the offices work together seamlessly. In his new role as managing director of Global Engagement and Corporate Responsibility,

Beginning in 2007, Edelman added several initiatives to improve workplace quality and strengthen Edelman's diversity. This includes an effort called the Global Women's Executive Network (GWEN) to boost its ranks of female senior executives. To date, the group has more than 700 members from around the world. Led by Gail Becker, GWEN provides female employees

Mark Hass, who first joined Edelman as president of the firm's operations in China, was named president and CEO of Edelman U.S. in 2012.

Gail Becker, chair of operations in Latin America and Canada, also leads the firm's Global Women's Executive Network (GWEN).

Together, Dan and Ruth blow out the candles on the cake at Dan's 90th birthday celebration in Chicago in July 2010.

with mentoring, training, and career counseling in an effort to increase the number of women in the most senior ranks of the company. The stated goal is to have at least half of all Edelman leadership positions filled by women by 2015.

"Never have I seen a reaction for an initiative like I have seen for GWEN," said Becker. "I didn't just get email requests from people asking to sign up. I received hundreds of lengthy, passionate, and eloquent notes telling me why they are so genuinely proud to work at a company like Edelman where initiatives like GWEN are a priority."

THE FUTURE FACES OF EDELMAN

The new wave of leaders at Edelman will likely include three young women who share the company name: Richard and Roz's three daughters, Margot, Tory, and Amanda.

After graduating from Harvard College, Margot spent two years in Edelman offices in Chicago, Shanghai, New York, and London, as well as on the press team at the World Economic Forum. Now, she is following in her father's footsteps and completing her MBA at the Harvard Business School. Tory, who spent a semester at Minzu University in Beijing, is finishing her undergraduate studies

at Bowdoin College in Maine. She interned with the Edelman New York digital practice and worked with the 9/11 Memorial Foundation during the summer 2011 break. Amanda, a high school senior in New York City, is applying to colleges and thinking about interning at an Edelman office next summer, possibly in Spain or Argentina.

Margot plans to join the Edelman corporate P.R. practice in New York after graduation, and Tory talks about the possibility of returning to China and working in an Edelman office there. "There's pressure with the thought of having to live up to the accomplishments of my grandfather and father," said Tory. "But I've also seen the joy they get out of their jobs."

Added Amanda: "The business also brings our family together, making us that much closer. It helps define us as a hardworking group."

"Is it a necessary that they all join Edelman? No," said Richard. "Is it desirable? Of course. I want Edelman to remain a family business. But as was the case with me – and my brother and sister – my daughters will have to earn it. They will need to prove themselves."

In 2007, 12-year-old Amanda Edelman posed in front of a street sign for Honorary Daniel J. Edelman Place in Chicago. The city renamed the street in 2000 in honor of Dan's many contributions to the community.

Three generations of Edelmans pose for a family photo at Dan's 90th birthday party. Dan and Ruth, seated, are joined by, from left: Suzanne Krohn (John's wife), John, Renée, Margot, Richard, Amanda, Tory, and Roz.

In a paper she wrote in high school, Margot Edelman gave an intimate account of her father's typical morning routine.

After finishing his exercise regimen and showering, Richard steps back into his bedroom. He dresses himself in his businessman's uniform – Brooks Brothers suit (one of his nine, interchangeable except for the color – navy, dark gray, and light gray) . . . a pair of soft Italian loafers (which he always buys in January during the post-holiday sale) . . . an Hermès tie (one of the many, all gifts from his mother).

Richard goes to his dresser to get his Swiss Army watch (bought duty-free at an airport) and his

wallet, stuffed with business cards, credit cards, airline cards, phone numbers . . . so full its leather rips at the seams.

Richard checks his watch – damn, he has to be out the door in less than a minute to be on time for the breakfast with the head of P.R. for Samsung. He hurries out of the bedroom. Just as he opens the front door he sees his oldest daughter walk into the kitchen for breakfast. How long until she graduates from college? Four years . . . and then another two for business school . . . he'll be 56. Still young enough to run the company for ten more years . . . until she's experienced enough to take over. Keep the tradition proud. Then Richard enters the elevator and goes to work.

ACKNOWLEDGMENTS

I would like to extend a world of thanks to Edelman for enlisting me to record its rich history, and to scores of Edelman employees, past and present (and future), for sharing their time and their perceptions. This was truly a collaborative project and their names deserve to be placed next to mine on the cover. The narrative was based on their information and insights. My apologies to those staffers whose work is not adequately featured on these pages. Edelman has conducted tens of thousands of successful P.R. campaigns over its six decades – enough to fill a library, far too many for a single book.

This book would not be possible without the supreme talents (and patience) of the Eight Communications design team – Donna Torrance, Johan Vipper, Dan Altschuler, Julie Powell, and Steven Fabrizio, as well as editor extraordinaire James Harrison.

Edelman senior vice president Amy Treanor inherited this project and ushered it to completion in record time. Viva Amy! The design team and I are also deeply appreciative of the efforts of Edelman staffers Linda Schroyer, Jon Silver, Jon Felt, Kisha Stokes, Molly Molendyke, Nancy Weltchek, Paige Savage Bloom, Michael Bush, Derek Creevey, Jenny Cogan, Carrie Miller, Ann Glynn, Charlie Campbell, Megan Woods, and Raul Perez. Thanks as well to Edelman alum John Avila of Avila Creative, Inc.; Matt Cimaglia and Allison Greenwood of Cimaglia Productions; and Aurelia Malacud for their help with the photographs.

Richard, Renée, and John Edelman graciously shared their life stories and extended countless hours of assistance. Following in the footsteps of two iconic parents is no small feat, yet the Edelman children have all carved inspiring paths inside and outside the agency that bears their family name.

Deepest thanks of all to Dan and Ruth Edelman, who welcomed me into their home and into their lives. Like everyone fortunate enough to know the Edelmans, I feel enriched by their friendship and motivated by their example.

Eighteen years ago, Edelman took a chance on a young P.R. practitioner, hiring him to open a one-man office in Sacramento, California. Edelman took a chance on me. And while I left the agency after two years to take another job, I've always considered myself part of the Edelman family. I'm honored to help the firm share its remarkable story with the world.

Franz Wisner
November 2012